Tə'nasəde

The quality and realization of overcoming depression
and disconnection with
total determination in stride.

CONTENTS

INTRODUCTION

It's been nearly three years since I've completely *felt*. As I sit here, contemplating—perhaps, I should admit it's been much longer than that even. My life has had its way of creating a vast amount of moments, resulting in beliefs that I may have been doomed from conception. In multiple ways, the odds are supposed to be against me. I'm Black. I'm a woman. I'm a single mother. I'm *broken*. However, once upon my life, I had a bubbly, fulfilled spirit, until. . . I didn't.

The funny thing is, I can't recall the exact moment I actually adopted any sense of disconnection. There was a time when I'd crossed a few short term goals off my list; I was feeling both stable and accomplished and was left with a sense of *Wow!* followed by, *Well, what's next?* It was due to possessing a high level of feeling the need to achieve. Suddenly, I awakened, and the absence of emotions had uninvitedly appeared. They were accompanied by multiple forms of depression and some really intense anxiety. I was torn between feeling satisfied and not feeling good enough—with pretty much everything. It was one of the most challenging moments in my life—the grayest period so far, undoubtedly. I was conflicted, considering my extreme thought process and view of everything in life to be *certain* or black and white. Perhaps, in my mind, I'd been placed in a chaotic whirlpool, one so intense that I couldn't control it at that particular moment. As a result, I wanted to give up, perchance give in. However, that just wasn't me, but truth be told...I almost did.

I was weaker than I had ever been. I cried without reason, had anxiety attacks left and right, was deprived of sleep more nights than few, and constantly filled with so much confusion. Still, in the mist of it all, I had to continue to wear the armor of what everyone depending on me defined as "so strong." Fortunately, being the expressive individual I am, I constantly admitted otherwise. I must have admitted that I was as strong as the big bad wolf who blew the brick wall down only a million times, but **clearly** that went over everybody's head and no one was really listening.

My friends and family were oblivious to my suffering. Somewhere between one ear and out the other, I was painfully alone. That in itself triggered an enormous fuel of resistance, sadness, and a fair share of anger. I instantly went from a well-known, descriptive, selfless individual to a selfish being. In whatever way, being under-construction allowed me the opportunity to choose me for once.

I've always been committed to being the understanding and big-hearted woman that I am—given that I've always considered those to be two of my best attributes. Simultaneously, I found those same great qualities to be my worst faults. More than often, I put myself second to *anyone* I cared about or loved. Taking on everyone else's problems—fixing and saving—

was my devotion. I would pour out so much of myself for assurance that everyone else's cups would be full, in complete disregard of my very own emptiness, only to later realize the hindrance to my own self-worth and self-care.

Sadly, I can remember thinking, *you're there for everyone else, but who's there for you?* Of course, there was family, friends, rooms full of people, and certainly the Man above. Nonetheless, due to my own incapability, subconsciously muting my emotions, and the lack of any connections, I just didn't trust anyone to be there. Besides, I was unofficially considered the "den mother," as I frequently looked out for and parented most, even at the expense of dealing with my very own problems.

One of the biggest misconceptions in life is painting perfect perceptions of another person's life based on their possessions. Nowadays, what is surface surpasses what's really within, insomuch as what we see is not always what we get. No one understands that more than I do. After all, I wore my struggles fashionably well. Seeing that, I figured—past the eyes—no one truly cared enough to try to understand me completely. In hindsight, I journeyed on to care for, love, and freely understand myself, wholeheartedly. Since then, I've learned a lot about myself. For a while, I succumbed to uncomfortable circumstances and inadvertently inherited family perceptions that controlled my journey. Self-sacrificing and the continuous chain of obligation were two main results that spring to mind. However, conforming as best as I knew how was no longer working in my favor. So, I voyaged on.

The journey has taught me some valuable lessons that I hope, in return, will help you. I hope this book will administer to your own guide for self-worth, self-care, total fulfillment, and a healed, healthy, and happier life, thereafter.

I can't promise this transformation will be easy. In fact, it was one of my hardest battles ever. On the inside, re-learning oneself and working to change what we've already accepted about ourselves doesn't come so naturally. Even more challenging is having to dig deep and revisit pain that has been concealed lifelong. It truly takes a great deal of courage.

What I have learned is that courageous people have much faith in God—a higher power—and in themselves. They are confident, passionate, and purposeful beings with strong values and intentions. They understand the struggles, the importance, and the capability to **overcome**—be it fear, depression, toxicity, trauma, hardships and/or pain. Simply put, courageous people are aware that life requires bravery.

Be Brave.

Be brave enough to accept, grow, and live in your own truth. Be brave enough to supersede all of the shortcomings placed within your life. Be brave enough to choose YOU when there are multiple options at hand. Most importantly, be brave enough to believe that you, too, are powerful beyond measure. Now, let's really talk!

1

THE REASONS OF MANY WAYS AND A FEW WHYS

There's this sudden, heavy, and extremely confusing moment in life when you feel as though you've lost full control, value, and the strength to press on. It's within those very moments that your ability to withstand hard times is truly tested. Perhaps, you may even experience these moments far more than those around you. However, fortunately, one thing promised in life is continuing chances to grow —from the struggles, all the pain, and those crucial overbearing moments meant to make you, shape you, or break you. You have decided that no longer will these trying times paralyze you. You are finally ready to conquer and recognize the power you've always had to pull yourself out of darkness. With full force and God's armor, you have the ability to constantly push through. For no moment has occurred that God has not provided ways to restore you. Understanding that life is truly a complex process —full of re-processing—and a long journey toward total restoration, I presume you've managed to reach a point where you've made the decision to take a leap out on some much needed faith. That leap of faith that aids seeking new direction for your desired brighter days.

Certainly, there have been numerous times you may have felt defeated, but clearly you weren't. Maybe you are torn from the past, unsatisfied with the present, and extremely afraid of what your future has to promise. Maybe, like me, you've thought sedating all of your emotions would be the safest barrier to minimize reality. For as long as you can remember, you've decided not to feel—in avoidance to actually dealing. Someone wise once said, "The greatest test of courage on earth is to bear defeat without losing heart." You have borne, and your heart is still beating.

In spite of all the damage, and perhaps some long durations containing many tears, your heart still is still beating. You still have a pulse. Let it be a sign that you certainly matter and your life still has purpose. All the good and the bad—both minor troubles and major traumas—have all been in preparation to create the very best version of you. Now, you are conscious that, despite all the trials and tribulations, the same cuts that have created the deepest scars have in fact strengthened your self-awareness in more ways than a few. You're hopeful that, even still, there are greater blessings placed in alignment with your destiny.

Prior to realizing that life is full of inevitable challenges, many more lemons than plums, you once believed anything was possible. Despite all of the hiccups, with much faith, hard work, and determination this belief is still rooted in truth. Anything *is* possible. Your future depends on what you choose to do in the present, not what is dwelled upon of your past. Your past is just that—it's passed. Now, with much courage, transparency, total vulnerability, and faith, let's focus on shaping your future. For there's light buried within your soul, yearning to shine, and things are projected to become a little less . . . dark.

Reflecting on an unforgettable quote by Robert M. Drake, he states, "You are only as free as you think you are, and freedom will always be as real as you believe it to be." This is your time to believe and be freed. That dark, imprisoned mentality can no longer exist. It's time for an eviction. Make notice immediately because this is your season for change, growth, and complete transformation. This is your opportunity to embrace the good, redirect the bad and the ugly, and recreate a beautiful, healthy, new narrative.

REAR VIEW MIRROR

One of the most important steps to take before you start your car, it's said, is to adjust your mirrors. The rearview mirror is a point of paramount significance. For those of you who may be unaware, a rearview mirror is a device in an automobile that allows the driver to see (rearward) everything toward the back of and behind the vehicle. It's mounted to the windshield of the front window to give the driver the ability to adjust the mirror according to his or her seating position, but ultimately, it's for seeing behind him or herself.

When I made my first attempt at taking the road test for my driver's license, I failed. With all the prior practice I had already accomplished, I was overly confident that I had "nailed it." There was no doubt in my mind at all. Ironically, at the end of the test, my driving instructor reported that I did not pass. Roughly, by three points, due to failure of adjusting my mirrors correctly and failing to shoulder check when turning left—all of which I had known and been taught to do. Yet, I didn't quite understand how imperative either of the two acts were at the time. A bit disappointed but in no way discouraged, I was pleased to announce that I was finally legit just a few weeks later. Fast forward through many years of driving, and one thing's for certain: I adjust and utilize my rearview mirror often. To be honest, I probably glance in that mirror twice more than the average driver. In a sense, I'd like to think that failing my driving test has conditioned my driving techniques. After any disappointment and/or setback, pursuing purism requires confidence, consciousness, and commitment. It wasn't till a long car ride to Florida, in the middle of a rainstorm with pouring rain and little to no visibility, that I could actually overstand such.

As I was focused and praying for the storm to pass, I adjusted my mirror and continued glancing back repeatedly. At one point, the rain was so intense, I could barely recognize all of the cars that were stopped with their hazard lights on. So, with a lot of faith, I decided to continue driving—cautiously thinking that, if I followed the drivers in my rearview, like them, I would only be stuck in the rainstorm even longer than I wished to attend. In total relief and with a huge smile, the skies cleared up and what seemed to have lasted forever finally came to an end. The *clever* decision to keep driving forward was absolutely successful. After a good ten minutes, I made it through and was finally on my way to my destination.

It took quite a while for me to realize the overall benefits of a rearview mirror. I had come to terms that one of the biggest problems with looking back was learning, simultaneously, that you never actually focus on all of what's coming in front of you. Over time, and with many different life-driven experiences, we learn there are advantages in seeing rearward things—yet, withstanding **ANYTHING** in life requires resilience. We have to put forth effort in taking decisive actions, all while doing our very best to avoid any negative outlooks of *insurmountable* problems. Otherwise, unfortunately, we will remain fixed and immobile.

I'm pretty sure, by now, you know I am not just talking about rearview mirrors, rainstorms and, or driver's ed.

Looking back at past mistakes, unhealthy situations, failed relationships, lessons learned—whatever it may be—is a mirror of strength and pure apprehension toward all the work and successful progress. It's total proof that you have made it through, no matter how little the progress may be. Although life is understood in many different rearview perspectives, one must commit to live forward, steer clear, and continue to weather the storms head on. It takes some time, a lot of strength, and even more effort to cultivate resiliency in your everyday life. Believe me, this I do know!

Even so, it’s imperative in order to intentionally grow.

WEAK FOUNDATIONS

Naturally, we take vast enjoyment in discovering all we can about the things we admire—who and all of what we truly care most about. If it's our favorite celebrity, with today's social media and just a click of one button, we'll follow their Instagram, Snapchat, and Twitter accounts, etc., to keep up with what and how they're doing. If it's a broadcast TV show, we'll faithfully tune in at its scheduled airtime. If there's a relatable subject, we tend to quickly take on a viewpoint any time it's up for discussion. In fact, most of these areas somehow become our own personal studies.

It's fine, of course, to have multiple interests and to dedicate time becoming knowledgeable about these specific areas of preference. However, this is where one should take interest and ask the question, "How can I properly navigate where I'm going and/or measure my growth, if I haven't fully comprehended where I've actually been?"

Take a minute and merely think about how you arrived at this present moment. Think of ways you were nurtured, your living environments, work ethic, the things, impactful events, and the people who have helped shape your young self—back then and into who you are now. Before successfully becoming the solid person you wish to be, there's a demand to anatomize every region of such. We literally have to know the basics before we can ever attempt to study the intermediate and/or seek the advanced levels of our whole self. Frankly, for most, this may require digging really deep and pursuing a complete rewiring of oneself.

Consider the following perspective: If your purchase of an old, fixer-upper home with an enormous number of repair requirements were equal to the present state of your life, would you renege? Would you dismiss the potentially perfect home you've envisioned? Or, as any optimistic homebuyer, would you commit to the renovation investments and ultimately reconstruct your dream home?

Now, I want you to think of your past as this imperfect yet perfect, noble castle only a queen or king could command.

- Can you recall having a fortified structure?
- Good gatekeepers?
- Secure inner baileys?
- Maybe one or the other, or none of the above?

It's safe to say that perhaps the majority—not all—of most of your unidentified, internal problems withstand simply because of the lack of prior family foundations and previously indicating generational curses—curses that are continuously built upon second-handedly and unintentionally. If we really want to see a better future, we have to first learn from all the pain and mishaps of the past. Not just your own but also both of your parents' pain and mishaps and perchance their parents'. Sadly, in many cases, even beyond that. Many of us are up against a lineage of mistakes. You have to make a declaration to yourself to be the change you deserve to be.

It's said that toxic parents tend to raise toxic children. Presumptively, more than likely, a parent internalizing pain, sadness, and/or any form of suffering will—in some way—raise or, better expressed, *project* their complexities onto their children in the same mirrored aspect. As the famous saying declares, "Hurt people, hurt people." Regrettably, these poor qualities are the prime foundation for what we each tend to as a result of heredity. They merely become our first homes—our noble castle's structure—and the subjective map of one's reality.

It takes a lot of attentiveness and twice as much patience to study *why* we are the way we are. Although there are many different revealed reasons and—possibly—complex backstories for your most weakened characteristics, two things, in fact, are also for sure:

1. The very first step to healing or overcoming anything is the decision to NOT willingly conform and become a product of your environment.

2. Reconstructing is NOT easy, but it's certainly worth the whole process.

When I was just a little girl, I didn't receive the love I needed from my father. I can't even recall one *daddy's little girl* moment, let alone a simple trip to the park. My mother, in return, gave me double the amount of materialistic things—presumably, in an attempt to fill the void of my father's magical existence which I only later grew to understand. However, I could never completely accept the conviction of having fatherless complexities, only because—in the slightest times when he wasn't present—I was blessed with a stepfather who stepped up, stepped in, and, even after their separation, is still here. My father couldn't tell that man I'm not his daughter, even if he wanted to. In fact, the title *stepfather* is an insult and a total understatement. In any event, I did not give credence to having *daddy issues*; I simply defined my personal complications as tri-effects—for I am the product of a very grateful yet complex threesome, figuratively speaking.

Nonetheless, over time, I have inherited some of life's greatest essentials from each of the three parents. My stepfather taught me the importance of nobility, perseverance, and integrity; my mom embedded within me principles of self-sufficiency, self-respect, and a great work ethic; and my father taught me the value of a dollar, for lack of better words. Having all three made for a very supportive village collective, and I'll be the first to admit that, overall, I've been blessed and am very much so a well-rounded individual due to their collaborative parenting. For whatever it's worth, I'm fully aware my childhood could have been much more perplexed. Nevertheless, with great maturity and seeking knowledgeable self-concepts, I now recognize the full worth of all of their good intentions. However, along the way, I still managed to become a victim of *collateral damage* with a debilitated and dilapidated foundation. I, inevitably and incidentally, of course, endured a small scale of each of their own internal pains.

What I have deemed identical, all three of my parents have suffered from a lack of healthy affection in many ways. In other words, throughout their own childhoods, they were all, in some way, shape, or form, deprived of the necessary affection of warm and secure bonds. In return, this resulted in disconnected and estranged bonds between them and me.

Similar to a large majority of *damaged* people, I, too, once fell victim and created many excuses of my very own personal detachments. A damaged person is said to be one in which highly affective circumstances, whether events, lifestyle, certain beliefs, and/or any form of abuse or negligence, has such influence on a person in a way that leaves him or her impaired in their ability to function in a healthy or effective way within their life in general or within certain major facets of life. I had always managed to discount my emotional damage, as I never really accepted the sense of abandonment because I was surround by multiple loved ones. However, more times than few, I've felt completely alone. The times when I couldn't quite understand myself, I never thought to think that my childhood upbringing had any cause or effects. That seemed so farfetched and a lot for anyone to process. In fact, the two do go hand-in-hand when conveying unquestionable actions or emotions. However, in no way does your thieved childhood determine your future nor promote justification.

Remember, nobody is perfect. Every parent makes mistakes, and most can't teach what one has yet to truthfully comprehend. Be that as it may, with constant observation, implying analytical merits along with pushing yourself to be whatever you once needed, you can do your best to focus and assimilate your own mistakes along with the mistakes of others. Doing so reduces the probability of repeating unpleasant cycles. Your parents may have committed all kinds of errors and blunders, but that's not what makes you who you are nor what you have to be. I'm sure our parents' errors may be the cause of many struggles most of us tend to exert throughout our entire lives. However, I also need to give voice for those who happen to actually find a sense of gratitude instead. Fortunately, we all have the same equal opportunity to be defined by our own choices, not nearly anyone else's shortcomings and/or circumstances.

There is no doubt in my mind that most great-intentioned parents have all done their entire best. Mentally note, in no such manner could anything stated excuse what one is or has had to endure. For some things are just inexplicable. Despite that, holding onto too many conflicting things will ultimately keep you imprisoned in bitterness, brokenness, and total numbness. Making the choice to address the hurt you have endured is one way of releasing those ill feelings, and with that the demand to focus on yourself becomes of importance.

You have to make the decision to show yourself some kindness, compassion, and certainly some acts of forgiveness. Forgiving not only who or what has hurt you but also yourself—because doing so lends itself to the possible creation of such a more profound and customary understanding. I'm compelled to ask, *do you ever speak life into yourself?* A positive tongue is a suitable action when creating such.

Proverbs 15:4 [1]lets us know, "*A gentle tongue is a tree of life, but perverseness breaks the spirit.*" Also, Proverbs 16:24[2] tells us, "*Gracious words are like a honeycomb, sweetness to the soul and healthy to the body.*" Both are scriptures that come to mind when I think of speaking life into oneself, as they both speak volumes to me, personally. Now, I can only hope they do the same for you.

I'm urged to share a memory I recall from a few years ago. I was having a conversation with one of my close relatives—my *sister-cousin* is what I call her, since we grew up really tight like sisters do. Anyhow, she had a very bad habit of saying really mean things to herself, perhaps in a way of expressing a few insecurities and or seeking my approval. Either way, I absolutely disliked that she did it constantly. She had a complaint about her appearance, no matter how many times I attempted to reassure her. It wasn't until we had this particular conversation, where I cut her off mid-sentence, as she was saying, "My face is so...," that something finally resonated. In the calmest manner, I told her something similar to the nature of, "You need to be nicer to my sister, have a much gentler tongue, and say more positive things to her pretty self." I recall her slightly smiling, and after a moment of silence, she uttered, "I think I get that from my mom." Neither one of us engaged further in the conversation, but I could tell that the conversation alone hit a spot and it helped in a very impactful way—for both of us if I'm being honest.

Speaking life into yourself does not mean you ultimately deny the reality of your current state or situation, but it helps aid you to refuse to frame your world around your current state or situation. Your positive words begin to frame the inner world you live in. Through those kind words alone, a shift begins to occur.

Take a moment and just be kind to yourself; speak some life into yourself in this very moment. Say some kind words out of your mouth right now.

Before we proceed and move forward, I would like to challenge you with a small yet impactful exercise. I want to challenge you to start paying closer attention to what you're saying about yourself, and commit to spending at least five minutes speaking life into yourself every morning. Try saying as many small positive affirmations, such as: *I am blessed*, *I am worthy*, *I am patient*, *I am kind*. Say them out loud, religiously. You're going to become what you continually say.

Luke 23:34

**"Father, forgive them,
for they know not what they do."**[3]

Every so often, many adults tend to *jump the gun* and are quick to get angered with a child for doing something *wrong*. Without the proper assessment and with primary thoughts, they assume the child *should know better* because, to them, personally, the wrongful act seems to be *common sense*. But...is it?

Almost, certainly at least once, we all have been guilty of configuring such assumptions. Not only with a child but also with one another as well. More than often, we tend to believe that what is common sense to ourselves should be the identical sense to our friends, relatives, and perhaps the rest of the world. In truth, common sense isn't real sense at all—that is, if defining *sense* as sound judgement based on our own experiences alone. For that doesn't usually offer enough information to create a reliable conclusion, no matter how large of a number of people can see through that same *common* lens of a wrongful, traumatic act, or situation. Perhaps, common sense is neither common nor sense.

You cannot point the finger at other people's shortcomings and/or their perspectives. We all view things differently, through different walks of life and different life experiences. With that being said, we have to begin to take initiative and steps toward forgiving those who have wronged us in painful yet ignorant manners. A person shouldn't be held in contempt for what he or she does not know. You cannot give any, nor all, of what you haven't first received yourself. For instance, how can we expect someone to teach us how to truly love, if love wasn't ever a subject in their own studies? That is a prime example of the blind leading the blind and another angered minute gone to waste. I'm fully aware that it's easier said than done, but you have to take the proper measures of agreeing to disagree without judgement and anger. You must learn—and be open to teach—through healthier forms of communication and attentiveness, all while exercising forgiveness in godly prospects. Not for *them* but, frankly, for *self*.

It's evident that in this shallow, egotistical, influenced world we live in, it has become easier to accept superficial narratives, discernment, and to conform quicker merits in ways to get even when mentally, emotionally, and physically wronged. Some may even admit that it is acceptable to be revengeful because it allows a sense of tasteful vengeance. Two wrongs won't make it right nor allow one to sleep better at night. You have to be more open to letting go and allow "karmic" retributions to stir their own course. In contrast, become quicker to being more understanding and more focused on your own deeply rooted pains and complexities—for that's a lot of weight to carry in itself.

ROOT CANALS

For the past seven years, I have labored in the field of dentistry, nowhere near the field I ever imagined I'd work in and definitely not for as long as I have worked in this field. However, I have gratefully accepted my position, achieved much growth, and, through many different dental procedures, learned many new philosophies about life itself. One such procedure is the infamous root canal. For those unaware, a root canal, in layman's terms, is a procedure in which the dentist reconstructs an extremely painful tooth by accessing the corroded root, then cleaning and filling the root in hopes to rebuild a much stronger foundation and a new asymptomatic tooth.

While many of us may never need a root canal physically, we are all in need of some root canals within some of our own personal relationships.

My first figurative root canal was with my father. As previously mentioned, being the magician that he was, one day he used his magic to appear with the intent to make amends. Eventually, I moved in with him, my grandparents, aunts—who were more like the big sisters I never had—and a football team of cousins, literally. At the time, I was 12, and the lost time between me and my father wasn't nearly my main concern. As detached as our relationship was, I was more happy that I was sharing a room with two cousins and finally in the presence of my little brother whom I had wished for every Christmas. Sounds a bit confusing? Well, maybe to clarify a few things, I am my mother's only child and one of two of my father's surviving children. My father's absence robbed me of the luxury of being among his family, including my brother. I had little knowledge of them; I only knew my mother's side and my stepfather's family. Despite the circumstances, one of my God-given gifts is the ability to forget, forgive, and focus on the present. At a very early age, I somehow managed to deal with life's misfortunes in a calm, silent, and dispassionate way. I was loved and, in no way, mad at anyone. I really didn't care what had happened in the past. I was living in the present and very much content in it, at least that's what I'd believed. What I failed to really understand, frankly, was at the root of a learned condition of pure suppression.

Furthermore, many moons had come and gone, but, for once, my father's presence was consistent—although, in no way *normal*, he and I began to construct our own form of some sort of a relationship. Well, truthfully, I was abusing the ability all little girls have with their dads to *get over*, whereas he accepted the fact, assuming he felt he owed that much to me. With no real affection and the lack of any thoughts to communicate what was buried beneath, we all continued to focus on the bigger picture: he was there.

It wasn't until I was coming of a much older age—maybe 17—that my father and I began to occasionally discuss more sensitive issues and concerns from both of our pasts. Very much understanding and forgiving, I simply found it in myself to see past it all. Recognizing the generational downsides, the both of us having deeply rooted pains didn't quite seem to be in conflict with what we were in the process of reconstructing, personally speaking. All I wished to believe was that there was much hope for a stronger, more successful emotional bondage. Unfortunately, one's hope [and another's guilty conscience] can cause blurred lines, stagnate processes, and originate total disruption —in return, creating reoccurring complications and pains. Go figure.

As any dentist can confirm, most root canals conducted have a high rate of success. However, some fail due to underlying, unforeseen, and reoccurring issues, which result in a much more permanent solution. At the prospect of every dental procedure, each patient receives a consultation—an assessment —and there are two recommendations given regarding the matter of a painful tooth. Patients have the option to invest in a hopeful root canal completion, or a simple—possibly complicated—removal is offered. Both options are presented to patients with the understanding that nothing is ever guaranteed; it's all a matter of what is in the best interest of each individual.

The same scenario should be applied to the reconstruction of personal relationships.

Often, within any relationship, most people limit themselves to merely addressing the obvious and the immediate problems at hand, which leads to only implementing superficial solutions. Thereby, this approach alone doesn't provide the long-term resolution to an underlying problem one may be facing. When you don't eliminate or resolve the root cause of a problem, the problem will just continue to reoccur. Fortunately, there are multiple tools you can make use of when identifying the root cause of any problem. One of the best of these tools is what I like to call the *root canal technique*. It's a simple but effective tool.

Although this method is a technique formed from a metaphorical stance, it can be applied to almost any problem you may be having within any relationship in life.

The technique consists of the following steps:

1. Identify the problem at hand. Hypothetically, pretend you're engaged in a really heated discussion with someone. However, for some unknown reason, the other person wishes to keep talking in circles around a particular issue. While this may be frustrating, try listening really closely to what's being mentioned, repeatedly. Then, take a minute to mentally unpack exactly what's being said exactly. The important thing here is making the attempt to widen your focus. Now, your ability to clearly visualize *what's* being said opposed to *why* the constant need for repetition, possibly, will provide a clearer understanding about the root cause of the problem.

2. Make an assessment of when and how the problem occurs. Supposing the *what* is **clearly** known now, begin to mentally make note of the possible reasons when and how often this problem transpires.

3. With proof from step 2, define some of the boundaries of the problem, and begin to evaluate the possible reasons responsible for it. For instance, every time you and this individual try to have a mature discussion, he or she interrupts you and starts to use aggressive gestures and inappropriate language whenever you attempt to engage or interject. Well, knowing the underlying issue when mature discussions turn heated and how this individual's actions occur could, perhaps, be the reason this individual avoids the underlying issue, doesn't know how to take accountability for his or her wrongdoing, doesn't know how to properly commu-

nicate, can't handle the pressure, and/or maybe the manner of approach is misleading. Any or all of the above may be possible reasons to the true *why*.

4. Begin removing all negative outlooks, little-by-little, until the root cause of the problem is fully exposed. To illustrate, speaking of this same scenario, try different approaches, settings, and measures that allow you both to feel comfortable and heard rather than targeted and attacked.

5. Promote, restore, and provide some form of positive assurance. This may include reassuring statements like, "I want the two of us to be comfortable speaking about anything, without the use of force or feeling dismissed." Get creative; however, be direct in whatever way you propose.

6. Construct a counter-measure for preventing that problem from reoccurring. Let's say, some form of understanding begins to conform—make an agreement that will aid in the solution to the problem rather than reverting back to the actions originally taken. In this particular manner, an example could be easily expressing yourself by explicitly sharing, "I'm getting upset at this very moment. Let's discuss this a little later," which allows both individuals space and, likely, a much more effective and respectable outcome.

7. Say a prayer, and hope for greater results.

All in all, given all aspects, no matter the significant level of relation, you have the option of investing your time, energy, and strength into each and every one of the relationships placed in your path. It's up to you—and only you—to make the distinguished decision of holding on or letting go in order to be a healthier you. It is very crucial to do so, for NOTHING in life unaddressed or unconstructed will ever get better on its own. It merely becomes a form of total destruction.

EXTRACTIONS

When the choice to heal becomes a priority, you start to advocate for yourself by understanding all of what you truly deserve, and you begin to properly demand what's important to your own well-being. Healing is focusing on leaving the effects of the past behind in order to focus mainly on all that needs to be done in the present moment to feel your complete best. In no way can you live in them both—you have to make the choice between concentrating on your future or being handcuffed to your unsatisfying past.

As selfish as the thought may be, the choice to choose self ultimately results in multiple extractions of some things, as well as some people. By definition, extractions are the action of taking something out with effort or full force. In Chemistry, it is a known process of selectively removing a compound of interest from a mixture to form more concentrated substances.

Similar to both methods, you have to put forth effort when becoming more selective at extracting negative habits and—for sure—toxic people out of your life. I know from my own experiences that it's extremely hard, especially when it's a close relative because there is no proper way to deal with toxic family members. Some may choose to handle this kind of situation by limiting contact, while others may choose the path to cut off contact entirely. In no way is this ever easy; however, a lot of times, it is absolutely necessary. There comes a time when you have to realize that, in life, we are forced to make a lot of painful choices—the choice of releasing valued relationships is a main one.

Regardless of how good you very well may be at focusing on things that matter, exhibiting all of your good habits, and leveraging your boundaries—if the majority of your time is spent dealing with toxic people in unhealthy relationships, you'll never be able to be completely happy, and you will never achieve the progress or change for which you aim. Negativity is contagious and can be very exhausting. No longer shall you allow these toxic people and/or habits to drain you. Consistently indulging in such manners will continue to be the main cause of your very own setbacks.

Have you ever had a really bad toothache? I've witnessed both some mild and more extreme ones. In analyzing, I have determined that radiant pain is much more painful than the actual toothache. Radiant pain originates from the cause of one bad tooth to the surrounding guiltless areas (i.e., your jaw, headaches, etc.), thus causing pain to seem as if it is within multiple teeth, simultaneously—which is highly unlikely. Nonetheless, this is an example of the principle of causation. One bad tooth disrupts the next and so on. It can manifest itself as a chain reaction: you can't eat, can't sleep, can't even think about anything other than the unbearable pain that ONE tooth is creating. Still, most patients choose to bear the pain out of fear of their appearance, needles, other traumatic experiences, religion, and sometimes financial hardships. There are a lot of reasons to conclude but—after all is expressed—only one solution still remains: eliminating the cause of the pain as the main objective.

There is no difference when surrounding yourself with toxicity, yet there are many who struggle with exercising such choice because, perhaps, from childhood onward, toxicity was a familiarity they became well versed in. Children don't necessarily have a choice of who they are surrounded by, but adults do. There comes a time when this choice should most definitely be applied and exercised. On account of toxicity being parallel to pain, it radiates energy from person to person. It's sad, chaotic, physically, emotionally, and mentally frustrating. You may be holding onto some people because of your image, ego, time—maybe even your own personal abandonment issues. You may fear letting go out of thoughts of another loss because there is indeed grief in doing so, and that's honestly okay. It just goes to show you care enough; however, it's worthy to care for your own well-being more. Cut the ties, end the guilt, and start eliminating the pain. It's clearly time to have some "teeth" pulled!

Now, that's not to suggest that letting these toxic habits and individuals go means forgetting they even existed. My suggestion, frankly, is that you become keen on learning to love these people from a distance, so a greater shift for self is presented. This means learning to take the necessary time needed to pour into yourself, while establishing actual space between you and those toxic relationships. Create boundaries that are much more beneficial to you—set in stone and not to be compromised. For instance, learning to be present but not overly extended may be a beneficial boundary for you to implement. This is a major form of self-care, and—in my experience alone—it's challenging, as the line between the two is so thin. However, there will be times where you may actually have to engage in these toxic relationships, so just be sure to protect yourself. During these encounters, ask yourself an important question: *Am I presenting old habits that are compromising to my newly set boundaries?* Your conscious awareness of prior tendencies may assist you when seeking the answer, and trusting how your body reacts will help you to navigate. Eventually, you'll learn that, even with limited access, you can still love these people—as love is not an emotion that can be shut off as easily as we may think. Yet, self-love includes knowingly comprehending when it's time to step up, step aside, or let go.

Letting go is a complex situation, and many may even seek reconciliation to guilt you with their manipulative motives. Stand firm on your decision, use discretion and good judgment, but don't be fooled. Pray for them, all while continuing to focus on YOU. Protect your inner peace. Free yourself, if nothing else—for nothing will change, if nothing changes because change happens by choice not by chance. It's time to be grounded in truth and ALL that's for you! There is no more room to minimize how you feel about someone or certain things just to make another person feel comfortable. You have to start trusting energy because it never lies. You just have to let go. No longer shall you hold onto compromised, dead situations. In no way should you expect everyone to understand. It's not for them to understand, and, in that same breath, no way are you obligated to make them understand.

I challenge you to make the decision to extract some toxic people and things out of your life, without apology nor taking the time to over explain. More than often, losing those dear to us is simply the cost we have to pay for finding ourselves.

Release yourself from the burdens of your past. Let go, and just allow people and situations to be. Don't look for any closure, explanations, or answers that may never come. Peace comes when you finally realize only your choices create your happiness, and your life is your prime responsibility.

SELFIES

In the digital age that we live in now, quick—detailed and cognitively processed—self-portraits have turned into a permanent fixture within our culture. There are many different studies that have explored and examined the relationship between self-worth and social media use in relation to these portraits. Like most ubiquitous phenomenon, between science and psychology, there's been a number of findings to explain the ongoing love (methodology) of selfies. Some researchers have even identified three main types of selfie takers: communicators, autobiographers, and self-publicists. Now, my question to you is:

What type of selfie taker are you?

When my mother became a member of the iPhone community, she had some difficulties trying to master her new craft. Truthfully, I didn't have the patience to teach her (repeatedly). Apparently, she's not tech-savvy and couldn't quite understand my aggravation; however, she's clever, and her grandson is just as bright. So, between the two of them, I had faith that one day she would grasp the whole concept. Besides, if all else failed, I was sure she could easily ask Siri or Google. In the intermittent process, she began to get the hang of it all. For she started sending emoji filled texts and selfies that were way too close up from every location you can imagine. Though what mattered most was that she discovered a new specification for her choice of engaging—with herself and multiple group threads—which left me evaluating my own choice of self-engagement. My mother had become a self-publicist type of selfie taker, the type who utilize selfies to document their every move. Her new identity was more than a little humorous to me, but it also made me realize many other reasons and motivations we have for taking selfies of ourselves.

A selfie is a self-portrait that allows each of us to capture our own beauty within various angles, sometimes with the application of enhanced filters. It's, roughly, a new wave of discovering how one sees themselves. Although there are many debates about whether taking selfies is the new *norm* for being full of ourselves, there is also an available language of actual self-exploration that accompanies it. It's merely a tool to feed and desire a better understanding of ourselves, provided in a visual way. I'm grateful to have grasped a deeper concept of this new fix, now rather than later. Most of us already go through life simply skimming the surfaces of our identities. That is, we all often fall short of truly digging deeper into our thoughts, feelings, dreams, looks, and desires. We must learn how to practice self-exploration before we can ever expect anyone else to simply understand or make attempts at defining us.

So, just like that, I started working on exploring myself, little-by-little. Discovering an autobiographer's identity by taking selfies to record significant moments. Taking way more self-portraits than I usually would, for my own archive, I made the decision to create a self-exploration weekly routine—very intriguing and simple but intense, like journaling my thoughts, taking more risks and trying my best to discover what I have learned while also addressing my major limitations. My daily practice of expressing positive emotions, like gratitude, would assist me, but it took honesty to start a self-exploration routine. For me, some weeks were better than others. Honestly, there were times I would even ignore the truth just for gratification. The process initiated a lot of mystery and many questions I had to answer truthfully, like *Why do I react to specific things? Do I use defense mechanisms rooted in avoidance to feel? Am I really guarded? Who hurt me the most? Where does it come from—childhood? My teenage years?* I literally found myself constantly reassessing if my mental state from my younger self was still suitable for the adult I had become.

A Greek philosopher and polymath by the name of Aristotle once said, "Knowing yourself is the beginning of all wisdom." How did he know such?

The many acts of self-exploration very often take a backseat to our busy schedules, which makes it easier to evaluate and judge everyone rather than discover ourselves. We're all aware that facing yourself can be scary. Regardless, real growth and success develop when we can sincerely evaluate self. I firmly believe profoundly knowing yourself is the single most important factor to happiness. It also entails everything you identify with. When I really became dedicated to knowing myself, I started analyzing my own self-portraits comfortably and noticed a drastic change in my work and personal lives.

You can start small and gradually create a ritualized practice of your own self-exploration. A few good places to start self-improvement activities, which you may consider, can be as effortless as:

1. Spend time with people who inspire you. It can be via podcast, virtually, or physically, but take some time to surround yourself with those who are influential.

2. Volunteer at a local organization.

3. Read personal development books, like the book you're reading in this very moment.

4. Implement an 80/20 rule to eating healthier. This may sound like I'm implying you consider a strict diet; however, the 80/20 rule is actually a healthier but less-restrictive eating option that doesn't always feel like a diet. Eating 80/20 is frankly a guide for one to eat nutritious foods 80% of the time, while treating yourself to your favorite food items the other 20% of the time.

It's a huge challenge yet sacred practice. Peeling back layers of external identity takes time and determination and requires a wider focused lens; all and all, though, it's worth it. You will learn how to love and accept yourself for what and all you are, and you will also create the blueprint for all else to scrutinize and regard. Most importantly, you will start a series of life's journeys toward self-guided improvement.

If your declaration for change and growth has been initiated with a communicator's perspective—that which consists of taking selfies to engage—you may continue to seek the opinion and permission of everyone else. Don't allow your new walk of deeper meanings to be conflicted by anything other than your own self-reflections. It's likely you may have reached a different level of self-development—perhaps before all those around you —and that's acceptable. It's time to become your own coach. What's good for you may very well be inconvenient for other people. Still, continue to strive. Become the prime example you, too, once needed. Take the vow to pave some new, positive, and effective paths.

2
WORK IN PROGRESS

"Just as sure as this book you've chosen to unfold, it was once in a state of partial completion and seen to be an unfinished production—a hopeful asset with endless possibilities. Its success is simply stretched on my faith and, ultimately, a much increased spiritual gain—all within the waiting period as to what it will become and what it's meant to be. And you know what?! I'm quite all right with that, for I have found much comfort living with more questions than answers."

When I was a kid, I thought I had my whole life figured out. I was going to be extremely happy, rich and famous, a model, a wedding planner [just like J-Lo in one of my favorite movies], married with lots of kids [twins for sure], and I was sure that my biggest aim was to take EVERY person in my family to Disney World at my expense. I was more than certain about where I was going. I was sure of who I was and what I was going to be. And...I was completely wrong! See, life is a journey of MANY EKG (electrocardiogram) waves. It is literally a lifeline of ups and downs, twist and turns, highs and lows, peaks and summits, that mold who we are; however, it isn't the highs and lows which mold us but rather how we take and handle all those different ups and downs thrown our way. It wasn't until life threw me a few asystole functions that I truly discovered who and what I am. For I am a perpetual work-in-progress in every aspect of life, and you know what? I own it!

DETAILS

It's evident that I never got to become the ideal wedding planner I had wished to be. However, somewhere along the line, I was involuntarily appointed the "go to" when planning many festive family functions. So much so that when my aunt announced she was pregnant and wished for me to be her daughter's god-mom, I immediately felt I had two shoes to fill—bringing forth the very elegant baby shower she had envision was the biggest one. Planning her shower wasn't my first rodeo; luckily, I had previous experience and, more importantly, creativity. There were many details discussed, and I wished to fulfill them in a very precise manner. Perhaps, a little more than my aunt, I just wanted everything to be perfect. In doing so, in a systematic and orderly way, I began to track what I needed to accomplish and make a timeline of deadlines leading up to the special day. Micheal's had become my best friend, Amazon was my distributer, and my living room had inevitably turned into a Party City warehouse. There was spray paint, fabric, and incomplete centerpieces everywhere.

The moment we chose the color scheme and secured the actual venue, a lot more excitement came with the idea of bringing the complete vision to life. With much creative therapy—rather than stress—the shower had become my favorite ephemeral project; I was making cute little tutus, backdrops, letter blocks, and constructing fun and memorable games we would play. On the day of the shower, I got my setup crew together, and we did our *thang* reconstructing everything from the table layouts to the major and minor details of all the décor. The end results were remarkable—there was rose gold, multiple pretty shades of pink, and an accent of cream, and inventiveness and thoughtful touches were everywhere. She was pretty delighted, the guests were all astonished, and I felt very much accomplished. The whole process—her vision together with my creative strategies—epitomized the progress of completion.

It wasn't until I'd received all the accolades and questions of how I'd managed to create this and that, that I actually took the time to step back and process the beautiful ambiance of the baby shower with my own eyes. For me, one idea led to the next detailed idea and so on. Before I knew it, it all had come together in a cute and unique exhibition—pretty much like most of life's presentations.

Steve Jobs, Chief Executive and Co-founder of Apple, once stated, "Details matter, so it's worth waiting to get it right." To this, I can concur; for that's one of the many important lessons I certainly cherish most in anything I strive to do. Naturally detail-oriented, I take that on as part of my identity. I also tend to apply this to the majority of life's aspects. Analyzing and applying pertinent attention to details are key powers to changing everything. From contracts, clothes, baby showers—even bettering yourself—paying full attention to particular matters is of significant importance. It encourages self-introspection, which is good for personal development.

The key here is that it takes lots of detail-oriented labor to get to the end results of anything, really. To become that person, all you really need is a bit of dedication.

I've learned that scrutinizing everything I see and do, even as far as setting another goal for self-improvements, definitely has its benefits. Many may believe by doing so, perhaps, one may be hypercritical or defined as a negative individual. On certain levels, I would possibly agree; however, sometimes, critics can just be misunderstood since scrutiny can very much be a source of honest feedback. Thus, you're forced to listen beyond certain things and, perchance, compelled to become more perceptive. This allows you to develop foresight, which is there to help you detect potential problems while culminating lots of data to conform a finished conclusion.

I often wondered about many different emotions I felt but couldn't make out any present reasons as to why I felt them. It bothered me a great deal and caused me to become even more self-conscious, eager, and passionate to pick myself apart bit-by-bit even more. I was in a state of self-referral, and I made a promise to myself to remain there. I became so fixated on examining and repairing my own heart that other people's opinions of me were totally dismissed, which was in complete contrast to one point in time when some of their validation was highly considered. However, with such dismissal, I was able to be freed from the outside noises and introduced to a higher level of self-dedication. That increased self-dedication came with greater details of many heartbreaks to wholeness.

BECOMING

There are many different feelings that occur when becoming a first-time parent. Perhaps, some feelings are even felt a lot more intensely than others. There's some doubt, sadness, much happiness [hopefully], gratitude, and possibly many ounces of fear. Naturally, it's the unknown facts and lack of experience that magnify the particular emotions of fear—above all else. Of the many lessons I was taught from adolescence to adulthood, becoming a parent is close to one of the last lessons on the list to be taught. More ways promoting awareness of avoidance were expressed more than anything. However, when pregnancy actually becomes something to accept, it becomes one of the never-ending subject matters to study. Although many books are provided on what to expect according to the advisement of prepared experts, you find that—no different from our own life journey—parenthood has no single correct and *definite* method [providing LOVE and changing diapers, excluded of course].

As I've reflected on the day I discovered I was pregnant, I've often tried to reprocess all the different emotions I felt. At that particular time, my heart was desolate of various warm feelings. In all honesty, I felt rather dark, inappropriately guilty, and robbed of such a beautiful experience. I was a few months shy of reaching a new decade [age 20] and literally in the middle of figuring out my way of life. It was my first year in college, and I wasn't even sure of my major, let alone having to accept the fact —that after six long foolish years—I was having a baby with a man to which I no longer held any emotional attachments. I found myself within multiple gray areas between happy, sad, and extremely upset, but I didn't have it in me to lean to alternative ways for I knew my child's life surely deserved a chance. I found it completely selfish, for lack of better words, to bring such pure innocence into a broken and unstable situation. That was one thing I couldn't have imagined or devised a plan to correct. I liked to believe that's the first time God laughed at me, and life definitely became really real.

Based on my less-than-picture-perfect experience, I didn't necessarily dislike being pregnant. At the same time, I was hardly a serenely, happy, glowing-with-the-miracle-of-life goddess either—I was more like a beauty within a beast. In no way did I ever doubt my capability to be an exceptional mom. In addition to much, much prior hands-on practice (i.e., babysitting), I had a lot of faith that God wasn't going to give me "no more than I could bear." I was fearless, however; I underwent prenatal depression—something I hadn't even known existed. It wasn't a severe case, for I never was medically diagnosed—and, by the grace of God, that mild period of depression didn't alter my day-to-day life or my prenatal care. Honestly, I fought myself really hard. It was a tough battle for sure. For quite some time, I had no ability to get excited about my pregnancy, and also, for the first time, I was truly at a loss for words. It was painfully difficult for me to express my feelings of disconnection despite it being such a miraculous time.

Whether becoming a parent or not, I'm sure you can only imagine how I possibly felt. It's hard for anyone to fathom unforeseen circumstances while concurrently dealing with the absence of desire and a tender heart. More times than few though, we are all forced to find different merits and ways to play the hand we've been dealt. For I never wished to sign up to become a "baby momma." I knew both me and my child were worthy of more than all the negative stereotypes associated with such. Yet, that's a matter I had encountered, and adjusting to being a single-mother was my ONLY choice!

You may be at a point in your journey where you have to painfully accept an unexpected life changing pregnancy (metaphorically speaking), whether it really is a baby, a career change, or a divorce—you name it. This life-changing encounter may seem like it has you down in a pit of darkness or full of confusion and dismay, with no light, desire, or courage in sight. You must have some faith and—if that's not convincing enough—buckle down, and make the decision to just push through, knowing it's the your only possible choice. You have to be willing to grow through it. Be *crazy* enough to believe you're *that* strong. For your strength is only built from the bricks thrown at you. A strong foundation isn't built by chance but by what we choose to become.

STRIVING TO THRIVE

Things continued to change when I had my son. Still on the fence about where I was emotionally, somehow I convinced myself that realization would have to wait. Had you let me tell it, I had bigger "fish to fry" and, financially, I was not where I was "supposed" to be. Between W.I.C and an overwhelming shower of gifts, we didn't want for anything for at least six months or more, for which I was truly grateful. However, always being hard on myself, I felt like I was in such a distressed circumstance. I was twenty-years-old with a baby and broken self-esteem, unemployed, and moving out of an apartment I shared with my son's father—which resulted in us living in isolation within a room at my cousin's house. This all made me feel inadequate and was extremely hard for me. Though it was the catalyst that sparked my bout of depression, living under those circumstances also brought me to fight much harder because, for me, being needy with a dependent didn't quite fit my description. I didn't like the feeling of being *stuck* and, in a sense, somebody's burden. The worst thing ever—in my mind—was having to ask anyone for help. Perhaps you share identical thoughts; your circumstance may even be worse than mine. Maybe you have no immediate support system at all, no dependents—nobody—just you. My advice to you would be to seek out local support groups for whatever support and any assistance you need. Also, allow vulnerability to become your main source of strength for there is much strength to be found in it.

Turns out, I can't stand being vulnerable. I mean, who really does? It's—for sure—my least favorite feeling. I hate it so much that I prefer to stubbornly suffer in silence, even if it kills me. Shamefully, I'm *that* prideful—sometimes, it's even hard for me to admit. I found that, times like these, I tend to disappear in order to better myself and to be the independent person I'm known to be. No one understood my isolation. I couldn't comprehend it all at times either. I learned that many people who choose to do most things alone have been through a lot alone, so they become conditioned. I was guilty of that. At the end of the day, I've always desired to be as secure as possible in love, life, and my future. I knew I needed to find where I could make the proper adjustments, and putting my pride aside was a great start.

It wasn't until I started revising all that was going on in my life that I began to recognize how each step was only preparing me for the next. Being so vulnerably exposed wasn't that bad after all; it allowed me to relate and reflect. I was learning it's okay to not be okay, and when you've been wronged, the only thing left to do is make it right. So, conforming to my own solitary confinement wasn't going to be my final decision. I knew better than hiding from all my problems—that was the easy way out, and anything really worth it won't be easy. Besides, I had a lot of fire left in me. I felt it deep down in my soul. I had to find MY pulse again; for the concept of the term, "A DIFFERENT ME" provided advantages for both of US (my son and I). I had to rise above it, and I was ready to live, learn some more, and listen clearly. Uncertain of it all and of what was to come, I just knew I needed some peace for my son and myself. There was no other choice but to get up! Giving up wasn't an option. I had a small pair of big, bright eyes watching me navigate it all.

God knew what He was doing when He sent me my boy. For there is really something about a bond between a mother and her son. I'm sure I wouldn't have loved a little girl any less. To be honest, I really didn't care the sex as long as my baby was healthy and happy. That he was. Semaj not only gave me a new purpose for living and served as my motivation, but he provided much color and a different kind of love when I needed it most. He was a momma's boy for sure and my SON-shine on the cloudiest day. Throughout all the down days and ill emotions we shared while in my womb, he was created to show me the brighter side of them all.

Together, we were growing. A whole year flew by and, with enough support, I had found a great balance between my studies, my son, and my social life. I managed to get two jobs and my own apartment within subsidized housing (the bricks). We were making due. I was striving and achieving all of the short-term goals I had set. Focusing on one thing at a time, I was finally starting to enjoy living life more, and my heart found some much needed inner peace. Fully aware that no one escapes childhood trauma—firsthand *or* secondhand—I was determined to provide proper balance and alleviate as much as I could for mine. I decided to no longer strive for perfection. Instead, I was thriving for a different level of genuine effort.

DETERMINE YOUR PUSH!

What motivates you? What's your *why*? Ask yourself these two important questions, then think hard about all the things that could possibly drive you to your new transition and the decision to move forward. When considering your motivators, it may be helpful to think of certain times when you were most excited to accomplish a task or a goal. Reflecting on that feeling of excitement can help you gain clarity on what it is that lights the sparks that ignites your flame and pushes you to do what you do. It comes in variety of shapes and sizes, from something physical to something mental—be it selfish or altruistic. That extra push and level of awareness is a powerful tool. It's the *why* behind the high level of engagement—that indescribable feeling—that transpires the answer to what motivates you. Perhaps, for some, it may take a little longer to configure, but the desire to seek is really all you need. Start small and simple. Motivation comes in all forms, and it's only limited by your imagination.

Two common things that keep us from taking steps to a healthy and prosperous life are self-doubt and fear! The two are unquestionably the most common roadblocks to succeed. We lack the confidence, become paralyzed and a hostage to a reality that is nowhere near close to what we love or deserve. Fear is fear, and there's just no reasoning with it; however, each and every last one of us has the personal power to choose how it's expended. You can rise up from any and everything. No bad spells of depression and hardships are permanent. You aren't stuck. I encourage you to keep going!

Remember that your hardest times often lead to your greatest moments. There are always choices. Choose one. I challenge you to create a new chain of positive outcomes. Think positive thoughts and positive results are sure to follow. Frankly, all that matters most is that you decide to thrive.

THE BEST DECISION

If only there was a manual, given at a certain age, that guided us through our toughest decision-making—perhaps then, many things wouldn't have such a huge impact when tough decisions arise. Who am I kidding? That's a long shot, and—let's be honest—the majority of us tend to make decisions based on our greatest alternatives alone, which is usually based on what is more beneficial than satisfying.

However, it's quite a mistake to believe that one alternative is better than another. For every choice that's made, there is really no bad; it's either a lesson learned or a blessing that has come to pass. Now, that's not to say that traumatic and shocking situations and/or extreme consequences are meant. Instead, it strongly implies a sense of some sort of knowledgeable gain. For these decisions help mold us to become the people we were wholeheartedly created to be. They help sharpen our moral sense of character, that is, when we can fully understand the power we have to create our very own reasoning—based on your value [opposed to others'] and your own deeply rooted fear.

Every day, we all have a common decision to make in life: get up, give up, give in or—like me—decide to really give it your all, whatever *it* may be. I want to challenge you to *just do it*! Take that leap of faith. I believe you can, and I know you're more than capable of succeeding. One step at a time is all it truly takes. I'm reminded of this quote by Chris Gardner. He said, **"Baby steps count, as long as you are going forward."** You have to constantly make the decision to push forward. Just look at where you are in your journey at this present moment—you have come this far based on the results of your own decisions and even despite any given circumstances. I'm almost certain there's always something greater to come from it all.

If you were to ask me what force has the greatest influence on all of our lives, my answer would have to be the power of choice. Unfortunately, often times, this isn't always known to be an evidentiary realization. There are many at a disadvantage and maybe in certain situations where it may feel as if possessing such power doesn't exist, which, perhaps, causes them to feel powerless when it comes to having choice. You may feel as though the power to choose is not an option at all, whereas it is one of the greatest gifts we each truly do possess. A powerful way to become more aware of your ability to choose is by paying closer attention to the previous choices you've made. Understanding what a decision does and the cause of a chain of events it can create helps aid in realizing the power of decision-making, and learning to trust your first instance—your gut feeling—is, usually, one way to help you become a more confident decision-maker. This kind of awareness requires intention and practice, like paying attention to your first thought in a situation and understanding what your gut reaction really is. You'll find that it's the only moral compass you personally have the power to create. It's the physical advocation that exemplifies everything you believe is right for you. On the contrary, we tend to stumble upon a mass of common decision-making traps that are possibly misleading and wrongful undertakings, such as anchoring, overconfidence, confirmation bias, or even as simple as making no decision at all—which is, frankly, still a produced decision. In most cases, that is the decision that allows someone else to choose what they believe is best for you. It's time you really start to think for yourself and release the need for these crippling habits. Strive to set your very own standards. Self-manage and start creating implementable strategies, the same as any other self-determined person. It's time you make the decision to take control over your own promising life. Besides, that's the best decision you can ever possibly make.

Even so, as previously mentioned, sometimes the best decision for us isn't always a great decision for our loved ones. More times than often, we don't even realize this until the damage has already been done. Believe me, I know that's a tough pill to swallow and often leaves one with an emotional debt. Despite your best intentions, somebody is bound to be impaired. However, this is where moments of discernment, sacrifice, forgiveness, and truth are forced to come into play. This happens to be a concept of which I just recently gained a much deeper understanding. A real *aha!* moment of acceptance, pardon, and a lot of needed peace.

With an open heart and very intrigued mind, for days, I sat back and really contemplated the many available categories of differences. Relationship choices happened to be one. I explored the differential factors of my most intimate relationships, as well as all the casualties placed among them. After a while, multiple thoughts of my mom had been heavily placed upon my heart, leading me to dissect many sensitive reasonings and some of her very own personal decisions. I reminisced on a point in time when I was literally her shadow and thought really hard about when and why that changed. I couldn't make the distinction between her sending me down south with my aunt or the time I was forced to live in the city with my grandmother [my stepfather's mom] for a year. Either way, I wanted to be with my mom, and back then, I couldn't understand any of all that I understand now. Forced to face some real truth, at the same time, I learned that all these years later I had quite some resentment toward her. Perhaps, maybe, I have both mommy and daddy issues. Furthermore, growing and seeking nothing other than peace, I've willingly accepted that this isn't about whether any of her decisions were right or wrong. It's also not another tactic to hide behind my pain. It's merely a prime example that my mother is only human. The same goes for both me and you. It is a step toward healing and a deeply agonized release. Whether I agree with any of my mother's choices or not, I accept them and completely understand her true intentions. My mom valued my innocence and all that I was subjected to the most. There wasn't any form of neglect, even though the distance meant seeing me less. I can attest to that period of time being really hard, and now it's a decision I can only grow to respect.

As you continue to read this book, you'll find there will be a lot of times where you are forced to face the same truth I once needed to face. It will be uncomfortable, as hard truths can cause pain and many tears. There are some things we just... don't want to know. These are actually the kinds of things we are usually already well aware of but would much rather live out our lives pretending we don't. I'll be honest, there are probably some choices that aren't any more exciting for me to talk about than they are for you to have to think about—such as conformity, acceptance, abuse, heartbreaks, and even addiction. However, the truth is that we have to talk about them, if you're serious about doing what it takes to find peace and much happiness.

I urge you, for a second, to dwell upon the main reasons for your push and the clarity you desire. Believe that you are strong and that you have every right to be brave. Your brokenness is the only true path to your breakthrough and God's willing grace. He has seen all the decisions you had to make and can recall the ones that have left you truly hurting. However, with strong will and that same God-given grace, you've gotten this far. Just imagine how much further you're capable of going. Be encouraged, and hang on in there. For your life's purpose will be the outcome of all your pain.

3
TRIGGERNOMETRY

"We tend to believe that happiness is a stroke of a special kind of luck, as if it is something that will descend like fine weather if you're fortunate. But the truth is happiness is the result of personal effort. You fight for it, strive for it, insist upon it, and sometimes travel around the world looking for it. You participate relentlessly, [all while navigating through many triggers and possible dead ends to discover within self is where it actually begins]."

Elizabeth Gilbert

It took about two years before I was provided the time to focus mainly on myself and my son. The different waves of emotions my son's father put me through were way too distasteful for my liking. I felt that pain in my soul for a very long time after battling between what was right and what was wrong with a bruised ego, a broken heart, and having cried many tears after six unforgettable years. Of course, there was the battle of who was *number one* because he was a really charming womanizer. There were far more lows than highs. I thought for sure he was my first real heartbreak, but then I'm always quickly reminded of my own father. The two had some selfish similarities, so, to say the least, they both abetted in their fair share. My father may have broken my heart first, but my son's father played with it the worst! In any manner, I always did my best to learn from my mother's, my father's, and my son's father's mistakes.

I made it past teenage pregnancy. I claimed second-to-none, and when I said I was done, I was done! I wasn't accepting no disrespect, no lies, and I managed to find more strength than anything in many goodbyes.

You see, when I love, I love really hard. I give it my all, with everything in me and chance after chance. For me, *sorry* no longer flew. *I love you* wasn't enough, and having a baby on me was the ultimate deal breaker. After all the cheating, belittling, manipulation, verbal and emotional abuse—you name it—that right there cut the deepest! Honestly, I felt that pain way too many times.

I never really pinpointed if it was the level of disrespect, deceit, or my own guilt from the little life I had to abort assorted with infertility and the selfish thoughts of *that should have been me.* Either way, it hits a different level of pain. It's a major trigger.

ISSA FLAG ON THE PLAY

I spent those two years regrouping, revising, and reconnecting with a little more of the girl I knew once before. She was fragile but so strong. Her ability to bounce back was out of this world. Very inspiring. I was proud of her, and she was content. Then, just like that it happened again.

I was minding the business that paid me and doing really well. Then, who I thought was really *the one* came along. He was charismatic and really smooth—so smooth, he manipulated me into believing he was going to be my husband. Emotional exploitation and mental distortion were his subtle choices of manipulative tactics. He was an expert in gaslighting, doling out guilt, undermining my faith in grasp of reality, and differentiating his words from his many wooing ways. I can recall so many times when I'd question his whereabouts and/or distasteful actions, and somehow, his answers always returned in the form of *because YOU* or *YOU never had to,* as he would attempt to convince me—in as many pleasantly mannered ways you can ever think of—that I played a part in his reasoning. He actually proposed, knowing deep down he wasn't ready for such a commitment. It had only been another tactical way to keep me on a string. I can't even say if there was ever really love between us or not. I do know he had a few ways of making me feel, and quite frankly, I was in love with the idea of it all.

At first, there was just something different about this guy. We had a connection that I had never felt before. We talked to each other without saying one word, and when we did speak, he spoke my primary love language. He provided many words of affirmation, and he had managed to get deep in my head. You see, I'm a sapiosexual, and intellectual conversations have their way with me. It was enticing and different for once...that is, until it wasn't.

I started to pay close attention to some common red flags and truthfully ignored them for quite some time because I was satisfied. However, being satisfied wasn't safe for me.

For a little glimpse of context, let me take you back to how I met him. There wasn't a real sense of romance, so no need for any popcorn. It was a regular summer day. There's this thing—when someone looks me in my eyes, I get the feeling they're piercing my soul. Yeah, that was it. I was very intrigued, and he once stated my smile had sealed the deal. He was checking on one of his boys, and I was hanging on that same friend's porch with all my girls. My son was present, clapping in his stroller, which presented a very strict line that was not to be crossed. I'm very particular and cautious of what's done in the presence of my son. However, this interaction wasn't my fault. It was nearing the time I needed to head home to get Semaj fed and bathed anyway, so I began to set off and started to say my farewells. I guess he couldn't let me leave without saying something. Respectfully, he asked who my son's fathers was. *What a way to go,* I thought. But I answered and didn't think to look back. A few weeks passed, and there he was again. This time, he asked if I was "so and so's" niece. Now, I'm a little reserved but very much blunt with a smart, witty mouth. I could tell he was doing an assessment. Comically, I had already attempted to do the same. I said something quick and slick, which led us upstairs to another mutual relative's house, and we literally talked until four in the morning. Very much surprised, I was comfortable and very open—and that was a big deal, coming from a very guarded woman. He was in a *complicated* situation "but single," was what he told me. His semi-honesty together with his overwhelming sense of humor allowed me to ignore that major red flag alert. I wanted to laugh like that every day, and for a year or so, I pretty much did.

Things continued to get deeper, and, before I knew it, two years had passed. I was in way over my head. One thing I didn't realize was how broken he was himself or the patterns I personally possessed. I was attracted to people I felt I could fix, which was an unconscious desire to save and rescue. I felt I could save him, even if that meant allowing myself to crack a little more. I had a lot of faith in him—in us, honestly. He had enough *potential.* I couldn't care less about the time it took. Now, I know time is something we can never get back, but my love was never measured by time; it has always been measured by effort. He was *trying,* so [foolishly] I stayed.

It wasn't until I woke up early one morning and realized I was only holding onto potential and my very own egotistical measures. I didn't like to lose. I mean, really, who does? I didn't want another woman getting my *prize.* I had forgotten that I was the prize. Besides, she had one up on me. I got the ring, but I found out she was bearing his second child.

Mentally, I was already gone. I wasn't fooling anyone, other than myself. I needed to remind myself of my worth, again! I had fallen short, as many of us tend to do when we believe we're in love. I'd given multiple discounts and allowed him to use his pain as an excuse for the hurt I was receiving. Faking smiles and justifying his pain were nowhere near what I deserved. Maybe I was far from clear when I stated the cost of my love. You should always know your worth, state your value, and never accept anything less. Perhaps, that's many of our greatest downfall. The majority of us tend to accept less and resort to settling or feeling trapped, at the expense of the many things we value the most [possibly out of fear of losing and/or taking major risks]. Then, the questions become *what do you value most?* and *what is it that you're willing to lose and live without?* Knowing the answers to these questions helps us prevent downfalls in love. For me, I had learned that I valued peace and clarity most, and I wasn't willing to lose myself over it.

So, I took a long look in the mirror. Observing my energy, I found that there had been a big shift. I began to reflect on prior identical moments, and my gut instinct appeared. It actually lingered for days. I knew it was time to trust the feeling. I had to remind myself that I held the power. Between the two of us, I was the smarter, more authentic, more transparent, more humbled, more loving, and more forgiving one. I had forgotten who I really was. I had to be real with myself. *What was I really losing? A headache?* Reflecting on the vow I'd once made, I was not about to lose myself—not again. Passionately enough, I really meant that. Those days were over. My son's father got the best and worst of those dark days, and, truthfully, that's what hurt me the most. The fact I was so vulnerable to share the life that was once snatched out of me—yet, he still took advantage.

I felt like a joke, but, this time, I was going to have the last laugh.

I didn't drop one tear when it was over. I actually couldn't even find it in myself to be sad. Very much confused, I was more relieved and, somehow, I found more appreciation in the revelation I had immersed. That alone allowed me to place more limitations on all of what I was willing to indulge, and at the same time, it caused me to higher my expectations. I believed that I still gained something, even though it seemed I had lost.

It's been about 6 years since I left him. I haven't had the urge to commit to anyone that seriously since then. Everybody I allowed close brought me such high levels of betrayal; so, I no longer had any desire to do so. I now had trust issues, and I was certainly misunderstood.

Carelessly, the first three post-breakup years, I played the game just as many men did. I did away with many known double standards. I started to write my own rules. It was my way or the highway, and I sure as hell wasn't hesitant on saying goodbye. If it was for me, it was for me—if not, *peace be unto you*. I decided, going forward, I was going to hurt any man before they ever got a chance to hurt me. Little did I know, I was only hurting my own spirit.

For a while, I liked having that sense of control. Nobody could tell me anything. I was desensitized and in a real state of rage, seeking some sort of redemption. I didn't care, and I didn't want to care. Once again, my emotions had dissipated. I wasn't as warm as I was known to be, and this time, I didn't think it was wrong. Although, deep down inside, I knew it wasn't normal. Well aware we are all born to feel, I knew the beauty that comes from it. However, I was set in some new ways, and I didn't dare to look back.

On many occasions our general decision for never looking back is rooted in the fact that we can't change the outcome. I had set boundaries and limitations for the people I allowed into my life but neglected to set any for myself, which I knew was necessary for further self-development. I was making many decisions from a place of hurt, fear, and insecurity—all far from the choice of strength I needed to revive my self-esteem. I learned that we have to be willing to analyze our fairly hard reasonings and be honest with ourselves, before we can ever be honest with anyone else. If we continually choose to maintain an unhealthy mindset, out of fear of starting over, we will never come to terms with our full potential regarding anything in life.

That's enough about me [for now]. Let's talk about you. Are you in a numb state, experiencing a lot of suppressed emotions? Many people will describe it as feeling an emptiness or despondency, while few will express it as a feeling of confusion or isolation. Some feel as though there's no future or hope for this rage of numbness to ever even fade. Not addressing such a state does more damage than good. Can you recall your triggers? Your fear? Limitations? Boundaries? Have you ever considered taking the time to reflect on who caused your lack of emotions or when they dissipated? I challenge you to take the time and actually think hard about those very few questions, then answer them all as honestly as possible. You can utilize the blank pages at the end of this chapter to get started.

Perhaps you have a difficult time answering, identifying the underlying cause, and/or recognizing the actual effects. Like me, you may have a history of ignoring the fact that you are emotionally impaired. Your emotional unavailability makes you fret, questioning if *better* will ever appear. You'd rather stubbornly lash out and run and hide the fact that you've been burned because, more than often, that kind of vulnerability tends to make you feel really weak. You might believe that admitting you're often triggered and scared to love, be loved, or to trust again isn't okay. More and more, this is an indication that the one thing we all really long for needs to start with a healthier rebuilding of ourselves. You have to be willing to express and indicate the many red flags and triggers that have developed in your life; for they have had their share of shaping your current mental state and are the main reason for all the bruises placed among your soul.

SHEDDING

As you dig deeper and deeper beneath the many layers of your pain, you will begin to understand how your current triggers are only evidence of past emotions.

There comes a time when we all have to face the multitude of issues that have made us feel the most incomplete. The way we begin to process all of those different feelings of inadequacy, while making attempts to form a proper defense against them, is critical in moving forward. Anything unwanted or unpacked, and any unnecessary attachments, hurts, and fears are the emotional baggage that must be shed in order to truly relearn to live.

In order to do so, we must become diligent in understanding all that has happened to us, all while knowing that all of what goes into our emotional baggage does not define us. Most of us have this striving desire to readjust the past and change a few things for the better because our reality looks nothing like how we want it to look. We have this image in our heads of how things *should have been, would have been*, or *could be*. This is what constantly daunts us downward, making it very hard to accept what has happened and how a lot of things have turned out. That fact alone has the ability to grow our sorrows, and those same painful emotions shape how we view ourselves and others. As we know, those undesired memories and emotions now have a huge influence on all that we seek in life and the ways in which we interact with people. Those painful moments create a blueprint in our subconscious minds, preventing us from taking part in new situations and relationships.

There are many variables that cause these thoughts to appear, but what we must learn to understand is that they aren't real. They have already happened, and your past has no business affecting you so much in the NOW. We have to learn how to release ourselves from the tight grip of worry and to merely begin focusing more on thoughts formed out of hopefulness. It's hard, I know. In all honesty, I'm still learning to master this practice myself. However, I've found that it is torturous to live in guilt. I'm often reminded of the serenity prayer and a scripture from the good book, "My flesh and heart may fail, but God is the strength of my heart and my portion forever," (Psalm 73:26). I had to consistently ask God to grant me the strength and much needed wisdom to accept EVERYTHING I couldn't change, while providing the courage for all that I could.

A STRONG CORE

If you are expecting for hurt to go away, you have to first start practicing healing with self-care. Start stretching yourself: your mind, your heart, your body, and your understanding. Try meditating for clarity. Try detoxing for a soul cleanse. Try holistic practices both for wholeness and/or simply being alone, to form a new level of patience. Whatever it is you hope to gain, you must learn how to create it in your own life. Rest assured, more will begin to manifest.

In the fitness world, we are well aware that exercising provides many health benefits and leads to some physical fitness *magic*. Whatever your age or level of fitness, there are no results if you neglect to put in the required work. Am I correct? "No pain, no gain," is a statement with which I'm sure you're familiar—but, are you familiar with what happens when your core isn't strong enough? Well, allow me to briefly convey what occurs in such an instance. Having a weak core requires all surrounding muscles to work overtime, just to hold you up. Many believe the core is just a sleek six-pack of aesthetic muscles. In fact, however, it includes a lot more than that. A strong core is about power, strength, and stabilization. Core muscles create a base for your whole body and allow you to stand strongly and firmly on your two feet. In physical education, one of the many lessons we begin to learn from grade school onward is that *health is wealth*, which has been proven to be very true. Challenging your core not only creates the toned look most people crave, but it improves a healthy balance, creates a great feeling of increased stability, and supports an increase in daily functional movements.

When I made the decision to *really* get serious about exercising, it was definitely the chubby tummy that drove me to the gym. I had basic knowledge on all the actual benefits of physical activity, but I figured a few jumping jacks was all it would take. Silly me! Jumping jacks are beneficial for sure, but I found there were little to no results where I had the desire to see the most results. In other words, jumping jacks did very little for my core. I still felt bloated and figured my stomach muscles were simply weak. You can lift weights and do whatever exercise you wish, but if you aren't working on your core and gaining strength in that area, you'll never be as strong as you may believe yourself to be.

Candidly, there is no difference with the cores of our soul.

When we experience a weakened soul, we know that a part of our living essence "hides" or begins to shut down. This hinders us from expressing and experiencing our true potential as human beings. Entire aspects of our psyches are completely repressed. The loss of this connection forces us to identify more with our egos just to feel whole again. Ego-driven reasoning becomes our survival mechanism, which becomes the main reason we turn to ineffective coping techniques or addictions. They feed our ego and a sensation of whatever is missing, and that sense of feeling temporarily relieved helps us get through that occurrence. However, simultaneously, we are forced further away from who we truly are and our soul is weakened that much more.

It scares the torment out of me to be this vulnerable and to share my truth in this way. The way we tear each other down truly worries me, yet I have accepted and acknowledge that I'm guilty of doing it, too [since I'm being honest]. Whatever shall occur, I know—now more than ever—sharing my moments of truth will somehow help many of you during your time(s) of despair. So here it is, and here I stand. Before I resorted to any kind of healthy, physical fitness as a coping mechanism, I often displayed tremendous swings in my sex drive. Hyper-sexual behavior was my preferred escape for any stressors I encountered. However, I had self-control and more than enough respect for my title as a mother to remain way below the spectrum of a true sex addict. That's not what I was. However, my sexual appetite led me to believe I could have been. It was my need for intimacy that served as a form of validation and encouraged forgetfulness of a broken place. Something was missing, and it was within the pleasurable pain that I was able to feel temporarily. At times, I felt it was compensation for my declined self-esteem, as well as my cognitive function. I was in control of my "situations," so I wasn't the one being taken advantage of—for that, I attempted to give reasons for proceeding, but I knew it wasn't enough to justify giving away my time and the most sacred part of me. I knew I wasn't right, and I thank God for His protection through the midst of all my wrongdoings. I was shameless, and there was too much convenience in it all. So, I turned a blind eye to that destructive behavior.

Now, I'm compelled to ask, *Is it possible that you, too, may be misusing sex in the same manner I have? However, have you yet to recognize this kind of mishandle?* Perhaps you are and/or have in the past but find it hard to actually identify your own patterns of sexual misuse, as it is spoken more of among men than among women. For me, I recognized my own ill-use when I noticed I literally turned everything into a sexual discussion and preferred sex over other common coping measures, such as alcohol or sativa. EVERY time I was in some sort of rage and/or unsettled state, sex was my vice. Eventually, my awareness of these many strong urges helped me view my behavior as my own moral weakness.

We typically don't realize that certain self-gratifying acts and/or ways actually are defined as self-destructive behavior for coping. Often, the majority of us don't really wish to address or say out loud what it is that's rooted in our hurt. So, we substitute the pain with certain things or activities that silence the hurt while magnifying a greater sense of feeling. Ultimately, this causes those same things to outweigh the pain we hate to discuss and derives a pleasurable feeling, like many self-destructive behaviors are known to start off. Three common destructive behavior's that one may possibly identify with are alcohol, drugs, and excessive eating. There is an infinite, complex, and broad category of behaviors one may engage in. They simply distract us from leaning in toward pain and, many times, most of us fail to do anything meaningful to stop or change.

It wasn't until I started to display some compassion and owned up to my own feelings that I really realized I was becoming what once broke me. In life, it's human nature to lean toward what's easier, rather than what's hard. That's with anything, but, the truth of the matter is, the only way to avoid not becoming an identical source of hurt is through honesty, seeking emotional intelligence, and having a positive attitude. It was hard, but I needed to be honest with myself and enhance my E. I. while doing the work to adjust my attitude. I had allowed my previous situations to change me in the worst way. It was all fun while it lasted, but I knew that wasn't really me. I needed to control that rage. That temporary fix wasn't it. I realized that, only after multiple engagements when I still felt incomplete and my soul was still tainted and weak.

So, I decided to go *ghost* and got heavily involved in working out at the gym. That helped me a lot. Working on my core provided the motivation I needed to strengthen the rest of me. I was doing much better. I started digging really deep and recognized some actual progress, as I continued forward in the process.

Some of your souls may be just as weak as mine used to be. Fortunately, there are many ways to strengthen it again. Inner work and retrieval practices, like mirror and inner-child work, are the best ways to reconnect with one's soul. There are a multitude of different ways; however, you first have to be willing to identify that you are actually experiencing some soul loss. Admitting the loss of your soulful energy is the first true muscle required in rebuilding strength. Own it. In no way shall you be shamed; believe me, you're not alone. Everyone is damaged. Most are just distracted. We all need healing—a really deep cleanse of the soul. In order to become more aligned, we have to first strengthen our core. *One rep at a time* encourages authentic development, and self-love and self-transformation are some practices you'll want to consider. For instance, when I first started my self-love rituals, I would Google small quotes, write them on small sticky notes, and place them all around my mirrors at home and my desk at the office. It was a small measure, but reading them to myself daily helped me build strength and got me through my worst days. Small changes eventually add up to some big results. You have to transform your weaknesses into your strengths and change your mind to work well with your heart, so they can revise a stronger soul together.

A HEALTHIER VERSION OF ME

One of the key elements of being the best person we can be is being the healthiest person we can be. Doing away with my short-term, instant gratification had surely proven that. I was in a very healthy place, and everybody saw it all over my face. I was glowing and had gained some happy weight. My thoughts were clear, and I was dedicated to pouring into my own cup. I was focused mainly on myself and my son again. I knew if I was healthy, he would be just as healthy, too.

After graduating from my trade school, I decided to further my education. I enrolled in Columbia-Greene Community College to begin my new journey studying psychology. Here, I began to learn more in-depth about how we are all wired and was able to gain an increased understanding and more reasoning of how other pains had transpired. It was very informative. Diagnosing myself and everyone around me, I was introduced to a much broader understanding. I was able to conclude that mental health was just as important as physical health, if not more. However, for the longest time, stigmas have been placed on addressing the importance of mental health within the Black community. I couldn't understand the shame placed upon it. A better understanding of all the questions of *why*, *if*, and *how* made me understand myself much clearer, insomuch as it persuaded me to take my own mental health a lot more seriously. Thus, I pursued yoga. I went to yoga class every Wednesday night for quite some time.

I was booked, busy, and committed to staying healthy. I'd arrive at the gym around 7am, work from 9-5, attend class by 6, and be fulfilling mommy duties by 10pm with and yoga once a week. I was focused and had no time for distractions or mistakes. At least that's what I thought, but—you know what they say—the devil knows how to work in some mysterious ways, especially when you are doing your best.

Occupying a repetitive schedule can get a little boring. So, along the way, I slipped and temptation caught me—but not in such way that allowed anything to get in the way of school because I was determined to complete that goal. I hadn't completely backpedaled, but I had begun coloring outside some much needed lines. I started looking for a sexual thrill, forcing myself to believe I needed a gratuitous *fix*. Perhaps it had been as simple as a song that had me in my current moment of heat, possibly even an alcoholic beverage that caused some sort of influence. The fact here is understanding that battling ego gratifications is surely a lifelong fight, and sometimes, you may end up "falling off the horse." Unfortunately, I had taken a minor fall. It takes great willpower to avoid certain behaviors, and I know I could have easily made the choice to not entertain the thoughts that led to my fall; however, I ended up making a decision without being self-assured and from a place of lack and, perhaps, a little loneliness.

"And I...Oops!"
-an iconic line

Reaching out to a prior long-term "fling" led me to consider a few rearrangements in my daily set schedule. I started entertaining him more and more, while neglecting myself [again]. I stopped going to yoga and substituted my mental healing for a much more intimate curriculum.

He was one out of the few who "understood me." Mistakenly, I let him in. I considered him safe. He knew most of my secrets, and I was crazy enough to believe we were some sort of best friends. I cherished the fact that he supported my dreams. He also agreed with most of my top priorities. We had a non-verbal understanding. We created our own system that I had assumed was working, until I happened to discover there was another player on our team. That was something he failed to ever proclaim. He had a whole girlfriend, and I...oops! How could I almost neglect to mention that she happened to be pregnant, too? Whew, chile! If I'm lying, I'm flying! Although I never actually agreed to commit, my feelings were truly hurt because this time, for me, had been a little different. Granted, he provided a thrill, but, simultaneously, I was able to show a softer side of myself. Just for that alone, I was bothered, triggered, and felt deceived.

I had a history of being very competitive [as I briefly mentioned before]. However, as I'd learned from both of my prior relationships, that form of hostile competition between women is very much an act of masking feelings of insecurity, fear of success, and/or unhealthy aggression. I wasn't *that* girl anymore. Remember, I was on a path of righting a few of my wrongs. How could I ever even try to compete? I was not about to gain that feeling of envy or the desire for another woman to hurt, and I wasn't interested in adding any more guilt or shame to my plate. Personally, knowing that pain, I sent him on his way.

Unfortunately, that was another bruise placed upon my heart. Although I never made it easy, I thought whatever we had was enough. I was actually exposing another place of vulnerability, and that alone was a big jump from where I had come. For months, I questioned how he'd secretly chosen another woman over me, which caused me to really understand that I had taken the cognitive leap in the direction of change because I was trying to understand some deeply rooted emotions. However, my emotional being hadn't nearly caught up at all. For whatever reason, I was reminded of my narcissist father again—perhaps because he'd never chosen me either. I managed to walk away from that break with more clarity and dignity though. It was another failed relationship but another lesson I needed to learn.

You see, we are constantly confronted by reality. God has His way of putting us through some uncomfortable tests. When those moments occur, we must make the decision to stand in our truths. I was loyal to my truth and started learning how important it was to keep firm. Regardless of how tall of a wall we may build or how tough we wish to be, we have to know there are some very delicate parts inside of us. We need to learn to care for them with proper nurturing, especially when times of temptation come knocking. If we don't learn how to respect every form of our own vulnerability, we can't expect anybody else to respect it.

I urge you to think hard on some of your most vulnerable moments. You have had a few, I presume? Did you choose to stand in your own truth? Or did you choose to do what was more comfortable for you? Can you identify some bad habits you may possess? Is there a habit you wish to change? I hope you find it in yourself to discover all of your silent, deeply rooted, toxic triggers. I hope to encourage you to truly dig deep and allow those emotions to come to a head. I hope you are able to analyze and confront them with grace and the strong willpower you have. Learning these triggers are a major tool in a bigger picture that you—as your life's artist—are sure to paint.

AND… ANOTHER ONE

At this point, I'm sure you can agree that love has had its way with me. It has exposed different emotions in a majority of different ways. It wasn't just the men I gravitated toward; I found it be the profound love I had for my family as well. Family is family, and that's just something you can't mutate. I cherished them so much, their stress became my stress. For a long time, I couldn't help myself not to stress. I wanted to make everybody happy. I was a real people pleaser, who overly extended myself often. I wished well for us all, but what I didn't know was that me pushing good for them was personally causing heartache for me.

I never really realized how much of a toll my families' issues and their lack of potential had on me. We were close-knit and raised on many old school clichés: *we all we got, one for all, and all for one,* and *blood is thicker than water.* So, that's all I really knew and what I vowed to stand by. Most of my family members have been my biggest motivators, and I thought I needed to work hard and be strong to provide and support all who mattered most. One thing I failed to recognize, aside from everything I would put aside to take care of them, was that I'm actually an empath.

On the web, *empaths* are described as people who experience a great deal of empathy, often to the point of taking on the pain and emotions of others at their own expense [which was something I did very often]. Imagine coming from a family oriented dynamic on both sides and being the most understanding. Yeah, I felt a lot, perhaps way too soon. I was burning myself out and didn't even know it.

We don't really realize how much of an impact or change is involved when different family stressors exists. Children change and parents change, hopefully for better. Unfortunately, in my case, the change that occurred was for the worse.

I found that I was becoming resentful toward the one thing I always wanted. For my own reasons [and the untold secrets of those closest to me], I never knew how naive I was. All I'd seen was the good in everyone because that's who I tried to be—to my family, at least—so it hurt to discover so much about the ones I held close. I was surrounded by the chaos of many addictions. For quite some time, nothing made sense, and I felt I knew nobody for who they really were.

Here I was, just an open book reading pages from each of their own stories. Another door opened to betrayal. It hit many nerves and brought so much confusion, but I still fought because I knew there was better within them all. I wanted to help relieve them in any way I could. I wanted them to be freed from their struggles, so I felt the need to help more times than often.

The thing is, you can't really help anyone who doesn't want to help themselves. You will literally hurt nobody other than yourself trying to do so. I learned that the hard way for sure.

One common thing many fail to realize, over and over, is that the main reason we struggle in our adult relationships is because how we have been programmed with unhealthy relationship boundaries children. Has anybody ever told you, *There is no one who loves you more than your family?* That's a lie. For YOU should love you more than anybody does. However, most of us have been so conditioned, at such an early age, by the people we trusted most, that we never recognized how our fundamental beliefs were poured with a lot of toxic ingredients. As we continue to grow, these ideas grow and lead us to many other relationships that are equally unhealthy. The truth is, we are not obligated to take care of, help, engage with, or forgive anyone who has not properly loved or protected us just because we share the same blood. You really have to understand that you aren't responsible for anyone other than yourself. Even those who bear children—there comes a time when you're no longer even responsible for *their* precious lives. You have to learn that it's okay to take care of you, and while doing so, don't ever allow anyone to make you feel guilty for it.

4
MASKING

"The most important kind of freedom is to be what [we] really are, [not what we pretend to be]."

Jim Morrison

Many who know me, personally, would agree I'm a *jack of all trades*. Anything I've ever attempted to do, I've always committed to mastering to the best of my ability. What they didn't know was that I managed to even master wearing a few different masks, hiding a lot of emotions. I promise you this, I wasn't always this confident; a lack of identity has been a main factor in my very own world, and hateful noise has brought me down many times, too.

MAKE-UP

"Yasss, Sis! Beat on fleek!"—that's what they say when your make-up is on point, right?

I can count on one hand how many times I have had my face made up. It's a very creative art but just not for me. A little eye-shadow and some mascara is all it takes. Yep, that's it. That's all. I'm reminded of my dear friend, who's a make-up MUA; she constantly mocks me, "Who just gets their eyes done, Nef?" Apparently, only me! However, I'm sure I'm not the only one, and it's not because I am opposed to make-up. It's really a beautiful form of enhancement, but I feel my best when I look in the mirror and see my natural state—and that isn't something I could always admit.

Growing up, I was the skinny, dark-skinned girl with long, pretty hair. I was the darkest of my friends and all my cousins. Due to some deeply rooted, psychological abuse, I didn't like that. I actually didn't like it at all. At one point, I didn't even feel I was as pretty as they all were. Living in America as a Black person feels increasingly difficult and alone. Now, imagine feeling that inside and outside of your home. I was the source of a lot of laughter and living in a world where there have been constant years of battles over what shade of skin was *in*: light skin, dark skin, mixed skin, etc.). The *shade* was real and a little tough to endure, honestly.

My grandfather was one of the few who were very instrumental in my beauty awakening. He provided a different concept of beauty, just for me. There's this old song by Sonny Charles and The Checkmates titled, *Black Pearl;* he would only sing it to me, and boy did that make me grin. It's a song based on shining light on a pretty, dark girl who's been in the background much too long. It's a song that definitely defined me. It was so relatable; I knew it, even at such a young age. I never had to express my lack of self-esteem, and, somehow, my grandpa knew—while, all along, no one else quite understood.

Although the jokes may have been innocent coming from my relatives, I suppressed those emotions for many years. I even accepted some backhanded compliments, such as: *you are so pretty for a Black girl*. I used to think really hard about what that even meant. After a while, the insult became a big peeve of mine, but, for a long time, I acted as if I never cared when I actually always cared.

That was one of the first masks I've ever worn.

You may have had to wear that same mask. Maybe even one of many others—whether related to ethnicity, homosexuality, and/or transgender identity, etc. Perhaps you've been left feeling unaccepted or unpretty, as I felt before, too. Maybe you've even felt identical to me. I'm here to tell you there's beauty in us all. With or without make-up, our shades of differences are unique and captivating. I want you to be kind to yourself and cautious of what and who you choose to listen to because words really do hold a lot of weight. Please believe me, there is a light in each of us. It shines for our own beauty to be seen. I truly pray you love the skin you are in, no matter your complexion, features, or the hateful noise. Sometimes, people hate what they actually wish to be; they tend to project their own insecurities onto you, just to make themselves feel better for a moment—whether they know it or not.

To all of you with more melanin than others, I need you to know that *Black Girl Magic* is real. I know it can be difficult, if it's not constantly reinforced—and sometimes, we are left to enforce it ourselves. Do it. Believe it. Embrace it. Always wear it well, unapologetically.

ACCEPTANCE

I stopped looking for the monsters under my bed when I discovered the biggest monster was within myself. To be honest, that's one thing we all really have in common. Quite frankly, these monsters all wish to obtain three identical things in life: to be seen, loved, and accepted.

For a few reasons, I have never openly expressed the ways I used to fulfill one, two, or all three of those desires. One, I personally didn't recognize what it was I was doing to myself at the time. Two, I found it embarrassing to talk about. Three, I didn't want to seem as if I was seeking pity parties. However, after really thinking about it, I came to the realization that there's really nothing to be ashamed or embarrassed about.

At the end of the day, we all have our own similar reasons. My question to you is, *who's really fit to judge?*

I used to believe that chronic people-pleasing was the only way to really be accepted. Making people happy made me happy, rather I wanted to or not. Giving made me feel as if I was loved because that's when I felt the most seen. I have always been a really thoughtful person, but, at one point, the thoughts weren't so meaningful. Sadly, sometimes, the only reason I thought to give was because it made me look better.

When I sat back and actually analyzed that mistaken concept, I found that some people deserved all I gave, while others were just taking full advantage. That made me feel even lower. However, it was there I realized real love couldn't be bought. For love is priceless, and if it is true, true love accepts you with all or nothing!

For many years, I searched for acceptance. Everywhere I searched, I never felt I was accepted completely—until I looked in the mirror and accepted me for me and all that I had and didn't have. I came to terms with myself, it didn't matter who didn't accept me without anything to give. I needed to accept Nefateria—flaws and all, big or small. This was hard to do, as easy as it may sound, since the results weren't as quick as the blink of an eye. Learning to accept all of me required a lot of "mirror" work, constantly sitting in front of the mirror and speaking life into my very own reflection. For example, sometimes, when I finished my hair and was feeling a little good, I would say to myself: "You are black and beautiful," "You are chocolate and divine," or "Girl, you're worthy and one of a kind!" It was weird, maybe even uncomfortable and humorous at first, but the more I did this, the more I started singing, smiling, and dancing until I liked what I saw staring back at me. It seems like a simple task, yet it is so powerful.

In life, we all want to be seen and accepted for everything we are, while [perhaps] getting lost in everything we aren't! Those who really love you for you will show it, and only after you accept yourself will you know it!

A LITTLE HUMOR

I'm sure we have all heard the saying, *Laugh now and cry later*. It's a common phrase a lot of my elders used when they were serious while making unpromising threats. My question to you is, *when was the last time you really had a laugh?*

Laughter is good for the soul. The scientific definition of laughing is, "a successive, rhythmic, spasmodic expiration with open glottis and vibrations of the vocal cords, often accompanied by baring of the teeth and facial expression." However, that doesn't really tell the story of what laughing does for us. The point is that laughing is known to be the best medicine, and I'm a person who loves to laugh.

Laughing establishes and restores a positive emotional climate and makes us feel good for a reason. What I couldn't understand though was why I always laughed to keep from crying during some real intense matters. I've come to terms that it is another armor of protection, way of masking, and a defense mechanism. Can you relate?

Whether I feel sadness, fear, nervousness, or an awkward feeling—anything that makes me uncomfortable or something of that nature—I tend to laugh from a place of uncertainty. I find it be a violation of my expectations, and it's a form of physical shock and an expression of denial to the situation at hand. It's merely a way to run away from fear and acts as a comfort mechanism to calm my mind down from a stressful situation.

Have you, too, ever laughed at an intense, sad, and emotional moment?

I remember getting a call that one of my relatives had been really hurt. As I attempted to express the nature of the call to the many people surrounding me, I found myself chuckling. However, I really wanted to cry so hard. I just couldn’t. That bothered me for days, and I even questioned my own senses. What I didn’t understand was how laughing was my way of distressing and trying to trick myself into taking control of an uncontrollable situation. That filled me with a lot of confusion though. I realized uncertainty is very uncomfortable, and I also needed to tap into pain a lot more. I needed to understand that crying didn’t make me weak, laughing wouldn’t make me strong, and hiding from the many different emotions we should all be able to express is completely wrong.

AVOIDANCE

Most of us go to great lengths to avoid pain. That avoidance, ironically, may be the cause of a higher level of much more pain.

When we experience any kind of injury, we begin to associate that injury with the event (activity and/or person) that caused it. Consciously, we begin to avoid that specific thing. Am I correct? In the short-term, avoidance may promote healing, but over time, that fear actually initiates another level of suffering, which leads to disability and [possibly] a form of depression.

There are many approaches for this model of pain behavior, and the majority of us are only familiar with classic conditioning and, perhaps, the fuel of this vicious cycle. Thus, our main choice is a game of hide-and-seek that we play within ourselves. What we fail to realize is that the best way to overcome all those fear-based situations is with exposure therapy and simply facing whatever it is that scares us. I know that's easier said than done, but that's just it.

I believe I've already expressed I'm a very straight-forward, blunt, don't *beat around the bush*, honest individual. More times than few, people have appreciated that about me. However, there have been times where my brutal honesty has caused some unwelcoming tension between me and some of the people closest to me. Now, I'd be lying if I said that has changed who I am or what I believe in because it hasn't, but it has forced me to become a lot more cautious with how I say certain things. It has also caused me to avoid certain discussions with specific individuals in an effort to avoid confrontation and out of much respect.

I'm almost certain all of us can contest to something of that nature.

I'm reminded of multiple times I have literally bit my tongue to refrain from saying some truthful but hurtful things to my mother that were in my head. I can even recall grinding my teeth. That compromised me in some ways because it wasn't like me to hold my tongue, and that alone has created many wars within. Both mentally and physically. In all honesty, it's a special kind of torture—avoiding hurting another only to inflict pain upon oneself. It says a lot about an individual. It also has the tendency to do more damage than good.

You should never allow avoidance to be the reason why you don't thrive in anything, really. Speak your mind, and be sure to speak it with your heart. Never cause a mess within yourself for any message that should be heard and felt! You were born with a voice, and I urge you to use it. If there's anything I've learned from not doing so, it's that it's quick to lose it.

PERFECTIONISM

Maybe I should have searched for multiple support groups. Perhaps, I should even start one for generations to come. *Perfectionists Anonymous* would be one to magnify, if I had to choose. I recognize this trait all too well, and being a perfectionist isn't always something to brag about.

Perfectionism is defined as a risk factor for obsessive compulsive disorder [which I am], obsessive compulsive personality disorder, social anxiety, workaholism, clinical depression, and the list goes on. Unhappily, I can identify with a majority of those descriptors, and I'm compelled to know: can you, too?

Sometimes, we tend to miss the suffering of others because it's masked in perfectionism and overachievement on the outside. On the inside, however, you see a person who *has it all together* and doesn't have a clue that they're actually dying on the inside, racked with anxiety, depression, or simply empty [despite what seems to be like the perfect life].

Perfectionist tendencies can surely be your biggest *weakness*. It took a real heated discussion with a close friend for me to realize it was mine. I can still hear her hurtful words loud and clear, "Yeah...but you have everything, Nef"—as if the multitude of my accomplishments should have subdued my pain and suffering, as if I didn't qualify to even feel what it was I felt.

That hit a real nerve but made me realize a lot of people saw me in that same light. It also forced me to understand that I had to keep moving past *perfect* and being a perfectionist really had caused a negative impact on my life.

Whether you are a perfectionist or one who has judged a perfectionist, understand that [more times than few] beauty comes from a lot of pain. You should never assume you can dismiss or judge someone's level of pain and suffering, simply by looking at how far they have come or their appearance. That's judging a book by its cover, and we ALL have a story to tell. Some stories just happen to be bound in a prettier book cover or tied with an even cuter bow.

DIMMING LIGHTS

Are you aware that life is all about having the proper balance in everything? I had finally found the proper balance between managing being selfish and selfless. I was literally "killing it." I was a great mom. I was taking trips with the kids, making time for my friends, and I even had some time for myself. I made time for family, myself, work, and school. I had grown used to being pulled in so many complicated directions, but, this time, complications were on autopilot. I was all for me and what made me smile. I knew I deserved it.

However, there was this voice in the back of my head repeatedly saying, *Don't get too happy, and don't be so proud.* Sometimes, it was louder than others, and a grain of guilt always resonated.

I started to realize it happened when I was in the presences of particular people. I felt guilty for being happy because they weren't in a place of their own happiness. I was dimming my light, and that wasn't fair to me. I played small, so they could be comfortable. It just didn't feel right to be happy and they weren't. That saddened me in many ways because, even at my worst, I clapped for the ones before me. To me, that was inspiring rather than intimidating—but we all have different perspectives, and I was well aware that it can be hurtful seeing someone grow when you aren't growing yourself.

I had to learn to clap for myself and came to an understanding that as I grew, some people were going to be left behind. It wasn't a write-off. It was frankly a fork in a road, and it only meant we were heading in different directions.

Perhaps you are at a point where you recognize that as you continue to grow, some people's true colors are beginning to show. That's okay. Just be certain to believe them the first time those colors are presented. Don't ever dim your light or play small. Playing small will only stunt your growth. Keep shining! You weren't born to play mediocre. If they get there, they'll get there; if not, you have to have the attitude of "see you when I see stylized you" and learn to be okay with just that!

5

SUSTAINING A FEW CHALLENGES

"Life is full of challenges, and none of us is exempt."

Unknown

When I was much younger, maybe around nine or ten, some of my closest friends and family members picked on me because I couldn't spell, even if meant my life depended on it. They laughed at how I pronounced certain words and witnessed my incomplete and scattered thought process. Let my grandmother tell it, I had some "thick skin." Most of the time, their hurtful humor rolled right off...so they thought! What they didn't understand was that I actually did my very best, and they failed to notice the struggle I encountered and overcame in the process. I never cared to share it with them, until now.

I often got frustrated and confused because I was very intelligent and had an extended vocabulary. My mom made me read the dictionary daily and learn a new word a day. Writing poems was my only outlet for self-expression at the time. To have a love of words, I couldn't understand why I experienced the constant difficulties I always encountered. Though I felt a bit defeated, that didn't stop me from writing—errors or not, I wrote. I was constantly told that I wrote very profoundly and detailed, too.

I suffered from undiagnosed Dyslexia and wasn't aware. I managed to do very well in school but that explained why I often shied away from reading out loud and performing word problems. It made perfect sense once I started to self-educate and finally expressed my concerns to one of my former English teachers.

Remembering all the times my mom spoke about "mild observations" but still forced me to read at the table while I soaked it in tears, makes me cringe to this day. That was a place of torment for me, but [as you see] I was a courageous little girl then, and that created an even more courageous woman. I've found it also made me feel as if I had to go to bat for those who weren't as courageous.

A desire to overcome challenges—both big and small—has always been my thing. I'm a true competitor at heart. If I had to bet on anybody, that one person would always be myself because, in my mind, there's nothing I can't do. I reckon that is one reason whenever I did fail at something, I felt it in my soul. I had to learn that failure was okay. It just allows another chance to get it right when given the next opportunity. I've always been ready and able to prove myself right, and that inspired me to project that same energy into anyone else who feared their own disadvantages.

I remember one summer day, all the kids were running around playing and had decided to do a relay race. My son is asthmatic and was among the few. He was so excited and ready to go. My mom—who has a bit of a control streak—came outside and immediately called out to Semaj, attempting to having him sit the race out. I couldn't understand her reasoning, so the two of us exchanged some words after she expressed her concern of his asthma. Now, I'm aware that asthma can be a very dangerous issue. I'm also very careful and take precautions. However, I was not going to allow my mother [or anybody else] to cripple my son because of a disadvantage—or plant any seeds of fear. As he started to walk over with his head held down and tears rolling, I immediately turned him around and we stood at the line together. I knew that face and the same space he was in within seconds because I'd felt it before. I can recall telling him, "Don't you ever let anybody tell you that you can't do something you believe in your heart you can and are more than capable of doing if you try." My son won that race, and he finished without missing one breath at all.

You have to get to a place where you do not allow other people's doubts and/or fears to decline, define, or disable you. You are capable of doing whatever it is you believe you can do. If you don't challenge yourself, you'll never realize what you can become. You have to believe—deep in your own heart—and trust there's NOTHING you can't overcome. For you are absolutely limitless, and that's one thing worth really knowing!

LIMITATIONS

> "The more a person limits himself, the more resourceful he becomes."
>
> -Soren Kierkegard

More than often, I've heard many of my relatives [mostly mothers] declare their loss of independence, in the sense of caring for themselves, after becoming a parent. Some even went as far as to proclaim their life was completely over. When it comes to time, we are very much restricted and restrained as parents. Still, I made time for ME anyway. My life was actually just beginning when I became a mother.

Of course, I have "mommy limitations," but I came to the realization that I'm not just a mother. I'm an individual. As individuals with a child(ren), we should still find time for ourselves and have constant reminders that our independence still does matter very much. Now, I'm aware this kind of time may look different for a mother with an abundance of support compared to a mother with little to no support. A mom with support may be able to take trips away, go to the nail salon, get her hair done, etc. Whereas, a mom with limited support may have to become a little more creative; during nap or bedtime, she may be able to take a relaxing bath, make a favorite dessert, give herself a facial, or even read a book for leisure. In whatever way, our sense of independence is even more important now, more than ever before, since we've become parents. If our needs aren't met spiritually, emotionally, physically, or mentally, our child's needs will not be met properly either. We cannot be our best parent selves when our vibrations aren't high in each of those crucial aspects.

I'm sure there are different circumstances for some, but if time is the biggest issue, you have to plan. Maintaining a strong and healthy independence with kid-free time is actually very important. It's important within any relationship, to be honest. You have to know that you matter. Limiting yourself to being just a parent, instead of a well-rounded person with hobbies outside of your home and the workplace, can damage the mental and emotional health of everyone involved. Maybe you have limited support, so you have no kid-free time at all. Try replacing bedtime for ME time every other night. Even if it's five minutes, believe it makes a difference and that YOU deserve it. You have to take the time to pour into yourself! It's very necessary!

We all are living with limitations. Some way more than others when we factor in culture, gender, and certainly economics [but that's another discussion]. For now, I'm here to tell you we are all more than what we believe. Even what we are projected to be is limiting, too. When we put our creativity to work, our innate ability allows ways to live around all of those same limitations. As a parent and/or spouse, we are able to find ways to create a "rich," healthier, and rewarding way of living.

I remember my great grandmother [God bless her soul]. She was physically restricted. Years before I was even born, she had to have one of her arms amputated. If I'm not mistaken, it had been her dominant side, too. Besides that woman's strength, there are many funny and wonderful things my grandfather has shared with me about her—but a particular, delicious thing I learned for myself is that she was a fantastic cook, and she loved cooking. I can recall many Sunday mornings, waking up, getting in the car, and riding over to her house with my grandpa. We would go visit her and pick up many aluminum foiled pans, full of a big ol' southern tasty breakfast spread that would be enough to feed our whole house.

When Grandma Jessie was injured, she was faced with a choice: she could have given up cooking since she only had her non-dominant hand to work with, or she could find creative ways [like her wooden spoon] to help her live around her new limitations, which she did. She chose to keep living and continued to have a rewarding life, anyway. It had been hard, but she didn't let that stop her from putting "her foot in" anything she had the desire to cook.

Allowing restrictions to take control over our life won't help when trying to live the life we truly deserve. Seeing whatever limitations we may experience as an open invitation to spark creativity is how we will live the life we truly deserve. You don't have to be physically impaired or become a parent to understand this lesson either. Focusing or conforming to our limitations, real or imagined, will only drive us to become stuck and cause us to diminish mentally and emotionally. Besides, nothing is impossible. We were all born to have it all, despite any amount of restraints. No matter what limitations you face, be creative. Become devoted and loyal to your own personal well-being.

DISLOYALTY

I heard somewhere before that, "Those who aren't loyal to themselves, can't be loyal to anybody else." Have you ever heard something similar?

You'll find [if you haven't already] that some people aren't loyal to you. Instead, they are simply loyal to their need of you and what you can do for them. Their loyalty may change, just as sure as shit—perhaps even sooner. Yes, it's hurtful. Believe me, I know.

They'll hide behind many smiles. Your accomplishments. A text. Even your success. They'll wonder what's next, and have the audacity to think of the finer things (gifts) that they can expect. All while neglecting to keep their loyalty in check—what blatant disrespect! That's just something nobody should have to accept! Somebody please, tell *Just Mike* I'm up next!

I really didn't mean for any of that to rhyme, but since it did, read it one more time. This time try your best to really dissect and understand it because it took me a while, unfortunately. Maybe I knew but didn't really wish to believe.

There's one thing about me: I'm loyal, even after you disappoint me. Another's actions can't change something I hold to such high value. Knowing that some people don't carry things the same way you do allows you to become much more understanding. It took a while for me to get there. It's been a challenge learning the difference between an unfaithful act and a disloyal one. The line between the two is really thin, but there's certainly a difference between them. Just be very cautious toward the people who disappoint you once in a disloyal manner—that may be a little preview. Act quick on treating them. It's the same individuals, so there is no room for any kind of sequels.

JOURNEYS OF DISAPPOINTMENT

Many times, disappointment is seen as a dead end. It becomes the main factor for why a lot of us choose to give up quickly. We often choose to conform rather than transform and create another way, failing to understand that sometimes our restrictions and dead ends are a sign that we're just at the wrong level. Perhaps, this level may require a lot more effort.

After some disappointments, many of us run and mirror a childlike attitude, similar to a child who doesn't win a prize in a game after hearing the words, "You lost." They associate those words with being a loser because, more than likely, that's what's been imbedded in their mental memory from the last loss they encountered. If we were to change those few words to something more positive—like, "Maybe next time"—that same child's attitude might be different from perceiving him or herself as a loser. At the same time, that change in word choice might leave that little mind some room to explore different conclusions for another chance at future victories.

I have a younger cousin, and she's a "sore sport." On two different occasions, she attempted to play the same game at one of our family's festivals. Her attitude was different after losing both attempts. The first time, she went and cried because multiple people yelled out, "You lost." The second time, she received a high-five for her effort, and most of us yelled out, "Aww, next time!" That time, she was okay with walking away, her head was still high, and there were no tears at all.

The thing here is a little affirming goes a long way.

No different from a child, sometimes positive affirmation is all we adults are actually missing. Affirmatives are universal and something we all need from time to time.

What do you do when you're disappointed? I hope your answer is simply: GET OVER IT [or something of that nature]. You can't foster the negative thoughts disappointment may cause inside. For that's just what disappointment is—it's challenging, but try again. Perhaps, try in a different way or with a more positive approach.

To avoid disappointment, we must learn to take things, situations, and even people, just for who and what they are. I know it can be upsetting when things don't go as we wish, hope, and/or plan, but that really is the best and only solution to avoid being let down and filled with much discouragement.

TRUST ISSUES

"If trust didn't require risk, it would be trust and without trust. Fear is the only possibility."

Unknown

Trust is so important in life and in business. It's one thing that is hard to earn but easy to break. Although I had been crossed way too many times, I thought I did my best to give any new relationship the benefit of the doubt. I tried to allow people to give me a reason NOT to trust them, rather than going into it as distrusting and searching for the reasons why I should. It wasn't until I had to identify with a boss of my very own that I realized I really wasn't giving anyone the benefit of the doubt. I was actually doing exactly what I didn't want done to myself.

In college, I took a course on leadership. It was in this course that I learned leaders and individuals in management positions should form a relationship with their team based off trust, while doing little to no micromanaging. However, this particular boss micromanaged everything, which was something I just didn't like. I knew my work ethic and was always one to get the job done, so I disliked that he didn't take my word as gold.

We had a semi-friendly relationship, and I actually liked the fact that I learned a lot from him. I just didn't agree with how he operated from a business standpoint. During a brief conversation, I pointed out his inability to trust; and he actually admitted to me that he didn't trust anyone because he didn't really trust himself at times. Considering his honesty, I began tolerating his ways in a different manner. I stopped taking his concerns so personally and became more proactive, having tasks completed before he could even question me. My efforts helped in minor ways because I would often surprise him with the unexpected by taking so much initiation. Whether trust was established or not, he knew he could count on me. My consistency had bred credibility and allowed him to understand that I cared enough, so our communication grew on a more personal level.

It wasn't until I became a manager myself that I had to revise my own way of operating. I couldn't tell if it had been what I'd learned from shadowing my boss or the fact that I lost trust in myself, but I started to notice I was mirroring some of his ways. It wasn't okay. I had to check myself.

I found that the challenges surrounding any lack of trust has two different roots. It's identical to a broken glass. Perhaps after the first time our primary glass of trust is broken, we learn how painful it is to attempt to put it back together. We end up hurting ourselves even more during our attempts. Somehow, consciously, we've concluded that it's best to throw trust out as a whole because it's too risky to fix. This causes us to handle the next "glass of trust" with even more pre-caution. Right before we know it, we end up doing away with glass altogether because we start to question our own judgement and our ability to handle it as a whole.

You have to be so secure in confidence and honesty that you're able to really trust yourself and your very own judgement—knowing that once trust is gone, it's a battle to get it back. Don't battle with yourself. Always be real, and stay firm in total transparency.

ACCEPTING IMPERFECTIONS

My whole day would be so thrown off if I left my house without making my bed. Despite how small a task, I would consider it to shift a gear toward a bad day. I examined my reasons of a "bad day" and started to understand that it was my perfectionist methodology that had been suffocating, deceitful, and detrimental to my life and even my success.

Succumbing to the ideal of perfection, you establish an idea that you can never be satisfied. However, I wasn't allowing myself to understand that because that was doing more damage than good. I learned the hard way that perfect isn't real, and I didn't want anyone to see me as perfect. I needed my loved ones to understand that I just wanted to be seen as what I was —all I had in that present moment and the many improvements I needed to make.

Now, I'm compelled to ask: *do you, too, suffer from perfectionism?* I wouldn't want to have you fooled into believing the process for making the previously stated improvements would be as easy as one, two, three. For as any other life-changing adjustments, please know that becoming a recovered perfectionist is hard work. It's a conscious and consistent process. Honestly, I'm still learning. Yep, I'm still in recovery. In fact, I've taken more time revising this book than usual because I wanted to make it, well...perfect!

The thing is being a perfectionist is suffocating. Often, it's a trait that becomes such a limiting behavior. However, there are ways to avoid and to help improve such behavior. Identifying standard needs, adjusting your standards, and facing worse case scenarios are a few ways to get started. But first, above all else, acknowledging that you actually process perfectionist behaviors is the main key.

I once worked with a doctor who would tell our patients, "Rome wasn't built in a day." I understood what he meant while trying to express patience to the patient, but I had never really applied that to my own way of thinking until now. Building a city has different sequences of events for it to become whole. It isn't just built perfectly. It's the same with our own lives as well. We have to build our lives, one brick at a time, all while accepting one imperfection a day and waiting patiently to be whole and complete.

That realization helped me understand that daily errors and all of life's trials together become our "Rome." It would be insanity for your expectations not to be managed accordingly.

We have to allow our flaws to be seen, and we must understand that they are the seeds that grow for something greater to transpire. We all are flawed and perfectly made imperfectly. I'm almost certain that not accepting your imperfections has driven you to a point where you've feared any form of failure. I'm here to tell you don't! Never lose sight of everything that takes time and effort. The only thing perfect is each of us living in the moment. Allow things to just be and accept that you're flawed, along with everyone around you.

6

SUDDEN STORMS

“There are some things you can only learn in the mist of stormy weathers.”

UnKnown

I remember the EXACT day my "perfect" world blew up into flames. It was May 30, 2017—two weeks after I'd just graduated from college and two days after I'd returned from a trip to Vegas. I remember feeling so refreshed and super empowered, even though the devil was doing his best work that morning. One of my good friends and I had gotten into a heated argument. Despite that, I pulled over [in an attempt to be a cautious driver] and parked to respond to a few text messages I had received during my forty-five minute commute. I was literally five minutes away from my job. Looking down at my phone, I never thought anything like this could ever happen and not nearly as quick as it did. Out of nowhere, a 4x4 pickup truck hit my car and sent me flying. In total shock, I couldn't open my eyes to see what it was that hit me. I just remember sitting there, screaming. A woman's voice said, repeatedly, "I'm so sorry. Are you okay? Please don't move." In all honesty, I was shaken up so badly that I didn't know how to move. My brain couldn't begin to process all that was going on, and I was far from okay for a very long time.

Something had changed—physically, of course, but something was different mentally as well. That accident took me out. It took me out of work and out of my glory. It caused my world to take such a huge turn. I went from being a workaholic to home-bound and in physical therapy three to four times per week. I was forced to sit with myself and my many, many dark thoughts. My love for driving was diminished, and a severe level of depression had rolled right back into my life.

I hadn't been anticipating such a huge traumatic shift, and I didn't want to accept the challenges that came with it. For challenges have the ability to knock us off course, and that's exactly where I was—completely off course. However, it was here that I was forced to learn a lot more about preparation. I also gained some much needed clarity about life overall.

Has there been a time where you were on a straight path and something happened and redirected your whole life out of nowhere? No warning or preparation. Not even one little sign to give you a hint? I imagine your answer is a strong yes. For life throws us one thing after the next, naturally. More times than often, nothing ever goes as we really do wish. What I've learned is that there are no coincidences. One thing often prepares us for something bigger or whatever it is we're supposed to learn next.

PREPARING FOR A DETOUR

In grade school, we are all taught studying is the main key to successfully passing all our tests. We are taught this sort of preparation is a very important step that helps us succeed in life, period. It's possible that we become so well accustomed to this way of thinking, we learn to plan accordingly for all aspects of our daily routines and future planned endeavors. This helps mold us into becoming an organized individual. However, my question to you is: *have you ever thought to organize and/or prepare for all the "rainy days"?*

Assuming you, too, have heard the common phrase, "Be sure to put something away for a rainy day." For I've heard that many times before, but it wasn't until after the crash that I actually grasped the real meaning of it all. Unlike the many times I've studied hard for multiple tests and successfully achieved, I failed to put anything away for any rainy day. My "security blanket" was nowhere to be found. That thought alone brought about much stress. The only thing I thought about was all the hard work I'd done to get where I'd gotten—then, it was all out of my own control. I was back to nothing, and the bills were still coming.

I was brought back to those same mirrored emotions I felt when I first had Semaj. I felt helpless, angry, and really confused. Somewhere in the midst, I began to recognize three essential concepts about life itself. One: detours are bound to appear, no matter how well you try to navigate. Two: no one technically has full control of their own life. Three: leaning on faith and seeking God are the greatest things any of us could ever choose to do.

Perhaps many of you are way ahead of the rest and have always taken the proper measures in preparing for the many detours and rainy days that may transpire. If so, I commend you. For all who haven't, I recommend you start. No matter how little. Create your own safety net; for nothing in life is guaranteed. I truly learned the importance of securing myself through my toughest time. That's not to say that this sort of preparation promises dysfunction won't occur—but it's better to be a little prepared than completely set back, especially knowing that anything out of your control can possibly happen. If and when it does, I hope, more than anything, like me, you choose to lean on faith and find the necessary spiritual alignment.

FAITH BOUND

"Faith is unseen but felt, faith is strength when we feel we have none, faith is hope when all seems lost.

Catherine Pulsifer

Growing up, I was taught to pray about everything [literally] and that having just enough faith would get you through pretty much anything. If I had something as simple as a test and I wasn't too confident about it, my grandmother would tell me to "pray." Whether it was due to the result of my own prayers or not, I can contest that prayer has worked. Many times to be exact. However, I'm also aware of how tough it is to pray when things are completely uncertain and your faith seems it's being put to the test. It's hard. Really hard.

Stripped from everything—my livelihood, my means of transportation, and my positive mental state—the only thing I had on hand was worry. It was during this period of despair that I was forced to learn virtuousness and patience.

During an interview with Curtis Jackson, the well-known rapper 50 cent, he stated something that has always stuck with me. He said, "You can't pray and worry at the same time." That spoke high volumes because it's the God honest truth. I knew that you couldn't solve any problems by worrying about them. You either choose to pray and leave well enough alone, trusting it will all work out in the best way possible, or you choose to worry, which usually creates much more concern. It's identical to the known saying, "You shouldn't cry over spilled milk." The combination of the two just doesn't mix. How can you really convince someone in a rut—a really dark space with no light in sight—not to fret or fear? The answer is that you really can't. You can only pray. Pray that the individual keeps the faith and holds tightly onto much hope.

Hope is defined as a feeling of expectation and desire for a certain thing to happen. It's a feeling of trust. It's merely a feeling of just knowing.

I have always had big hopes. I have always felt that feeling of trust. Throughout all the bad, I have always known that everything was going to work itself out one way or another. However, not during this specific period of time. This time was different. In all honesty, this particular time had been the hardest. I'd like to believe it was the fact that I had lost my total sense of control. I felt completely robbed. I was brought down to my lowest point ever. It was a pause on literally everything, and I was forced to start all over; I couldn't fathom that idea. My faith and all my high hopes were gone. I remember laying on my couch, thinking I wasn't going to make it out of the dark space that held me captive. I thought, *This is it. It's time to give in.* I just couldn't manage. It was here that I found I wasn't so strong after all.

Whatever you're experiencing in this present moment that has your life on pause, I need you to know that, even though it may be very painful, uncertain, and dark, it's necessary. It's necessary for the next level to which you're going to be introduced. It's necessary for the next level of strength you're being prepared to unlock. I'll be honest, I couldn't see past that; and I definitely couldn't understand. I'm sure your thoughts are identical. I'm here to tell you, "Don't lose hope. Continue to let your faith run deep."

I'M NOT OKAY

Days turned into weeks, and weeks turned into months way before I knew it. Nothing was changing. Everything actually started to get worse. My pain level, my tolerance, my mental state, and even my spirit were all declining. Out of much anger and pain, I had become really mean and beyond frustrated. My positive attitude had been adjusted and reflected all the dysfunction I was currently going through.

One thing that brought me even more over the edge was the fact that I was going through all of these different emotions alone. Given my pridefulness, I'm aware I have to take some fault in that reasoning. However, at my lowest and darkest time, my closest family and friends still figured I was fine. Nobody understood the type of support I needed. They were so used to painting me as "the strong Black woman," which was the main problem.

Being "strong" is why my pain wasn't taken seriously. Being "strong" is why I often received less empathy from anyone. Being "strong" is why I was the first person everyone called but the last one to anyone considered. They always believed "she got it" and that I could "handle it"—whatever *it* was. Many felt defining me as "strong" was a compliment, but for me, ironically, being "strong" became my biggest measure of hurt.

Often times, circumstances force us to be what we need to be in order to survive. As human beings, we are hard-wired for such. This means whatever our bodies and minds have to do to make sure we stay alive, our bodies and minds will do it. Fighting, protecting, and/or staying grounded have always been my body's first responses. I'm almost certain that's where and how my "strong" identity has been impressed upon me. I have managed to handle many situations in what seems to be in an effortless way—ways those around me would have probably never thought they could have endured. While this may be admirable, it's also abrasive. For we as human beings all experience moments of weakness, and I urge you to voice when you do [if this same identity has been impressed upon you]. If not, check on those whom you may consider to identify as such because it matters a lot.

I remember one day I was having one of my really tough days. It was one of those days where I couldn't even manage to get up. I was stuck in the fetal position on my couch with so many emotions. As I searched the web, I came across a video about depression. The video described me and exactly how I felt. As it brought tears to my eyes, I forwarded that video to everyone I could think of with a message attached, stating, "This is so me." I figured since I couldn't put it in my own words, the video spoke volumes for itself.

Some received it, and some didn't dare think to reply. My mom called. My grandma sent a prayer. I received many "I love you" messages, but no one showed up. That hurt deeply. That was the day I realized I had to be the one to show up for me. I didn't doubt that people cared, and I wasn't looking for anyone to save me. I just needed somebody to be close! Sadly, they weren't. I cried. I cried, really hard. When I picked my head up, my son was awake and standing right in front of me. We didn't exchange our regular morning affirmations. Neither one of us actually said a word. He opened his arms and just hugged me. He hugged me really tight! I knew he didn't understand, but he felt me. That was enough.

I gained so much empowerment in that hug. Experiencing that emotional connection was a revelation of who I needed to put first and what my true motivation really needed to be. That was the first time I had allowed my son to see me cry. I didn't think to hide it. I needed him to see that his mom is powerful, but that sometimes she's going to be fragile, too.

Revealing your pain is a really tough thing to do. Some people don't understand how hard it is to be vulnerable when everyone around you has deemed you as strong. It's one of the hardest things ever! I hope this chapter challenges you to vocally express and reveal your pain anyway. Express yourself to those you feel you can trust the most—possibly someone who has once made you feel safe and secure [like a mentor] or someone who has held some of your dearest secrets. Just be sure to seek someone who will certainly be honest and remind you that it's okay to not be okay and certainly not so strong. You have to know that. That's actually something we, as a collective, need to begin to normalize, especially in the Black community. We all feel it but have conformed to cope very differently. Many of us run and hide, bearing constant pain for years in avoidance of being judged or dismissed. Believe me, I truly understand. However, this does more damage than good. I urge you to keep openly expressing yourself in a healthy manner. Do it, even if you're left to become your own support system. Don't wait on others to show up for you. Show up for yourself, starting today!

I'M REALLY TRYING

Slowly, I started showing up for myself and made constant attempts to come up out of that dark hole. I knew I had to at least try. I didn't want to take the risk of making my son feel even remotely similar to the way I had been feeling.

I had secluded myself altogether because I believed depression was contagious. I wouldn't wish it on my worst enemy, let alone anyone I loved. Depression is really real!

Unfortunately, the best and only medicine is time. So, I was faking it to make it throughout the day. Seeking advice from my primary doctor was beneficial in some ways, but he continued to push wanting to prescribe me pills I wasn't willing to take. He also recommended I seek a therapist, which I had begun to look for already. The problem was I couldn't find one I felt could relate to my cultural background, which was as aspect that was very important to me.

You probably wouldn't believe me if I told you I decided to counsel myself. In fact, I really did. You, too, can try some beginner's work yourself. Please note and consider this as a disclaimer: I am not a licensed therapist and do not hold the proper degrees to state the overall knowledge required. I highly urge you to seek professional help if needed, if you have the resources and access. I'm only here to fully encourage and recommend, as there are many YouTube channels, webinars, and self-help books you can buy to assist generally. Also, there are certain podcasts you can listen to and begin to challenge yourself with certain takeaways while listening.

I remember buying a clipboard and all. I started to mock various therapy sessions I had found online. I started doing assessments on my daily emotional tank. There were "good days" and "bad days." Good days were normal, when I felt somewhat revived. Bad days, however, included a feeling of overwhelming sadness mixed with some bitterness that didn't necessarily have a root or a given explanation.

Like anything, it wasn't easy at all. I still battled with myself constantly, but I was proud that I was trying to find me again.

Where did she go?

Do you know what's worse than being depressed? The feeling of being completely numb to any feelings at all. Although I was trying to climb out of that dark pit, I found there were no real improvements. Nothing was happening, at least not fast enough. That alone caused me to fall into that numb place once again. This time I was in really deep. I was careless with just about everything. I couldn't concentrate, sleep, or connect with anything or anyone.

It was a scary feeling, and I vividly remember thinking I wasn't ever going to find myself again. The feelings I had been slightly familiar with had escalated to a height they had never reached before.

It wasn't normal to feel how I felt on a daily basis. I really couldn't recognize myself at all. I was becoming a stranger in my own home and to my friends and family. They didn't understand what I was going through, and I was tired of trying to explain it to them.

I remember receiving a text message from one of my close friends that read something to the nature of, "Where's my best friend? I really miss who you used to be before you became so dark." In a fit of rage, I recall replying something like, "She's dead." In all honesty, that version of me really was deceased.

It may sound very strange and unwelcoming, but sometimes you have to die inside in order to be reborn again. Once I grasped that concept, I began to understand the unfortunate opportunity I had been presented with. That whole traumatic experience had been a real eye opener and, simultaneously, a blessing in disguise. I just hated that it took so long for me to actually realize it. For sure, I was stripped of everything I had worked so hard to build in a material world, but I needed to be renewed on the inside. Internally, I needed to do the proper work to come back as a wiser, stronger, and more humbled version of myself.

I had to reintroduce myself to myself.

You, too, may have experienced an unfortunate circumstance. Perhaps you're just as "dead" as I was on the inside, but you have yet to grasp the bigger meaning behind it all. I want to challenge you to look a little closer. Try to find the blessing in the lesson that you're truly missing. Try digging deep in search for a different version of yourself.

EMPTY TANKS

My fuel levels were all on empty. I hadn't been full or felt good in such a very long time. All of my primal emotions had been neglected, and that was the main reason I hadn't felt alive for almost a year. However, I was pushing through. I hadn't given up completely. Every day, I started telling myself that I couldn't.

I needed to be refueled, one way or another.

I woke up one morning and, just like that, I didn't want to feel so badly anymore. I remember lying in bed super depressed. I was literally talking to myself. I told myself, "Are you just going to continue to sit here and do nothing? Are you accepting your circumstances for what they are? Are you letting depression defeat you? What about your son? What kind of example are you setting for him? If you can't do it for yourself at least get up for him!" That day, I ignited my push. Despite what the doctors had to report, I started to rewire my own mind and rebuild my physical strength. I started speaking more positive affirmations into existence daily, and I didn't need to take any medication to assist me in doing so. I knew the power of my mind and started to believe it again.

I got back out there and started looking for new employment. I quickly found one within walking distance which was truly a blessing because I'd had my first anxiety attack while behind the wheel just a few weeks prior. I was still dealing with PTSD from the accident, and I wasn't ready to get on the road quite yet. Working nearby was okay because I didn't mind walking.

Walking promoted exercise, which helped improve my mood and supported my body's stress management. It also provided some time to take in some much needed fresh air, all while listening to some soulful music. I had a true love for music, but I couldn't feel the rhythm to any beat for a while.

My first day back to work had me feeling like a kid again. It brought back memories of all my first days back to school. I woke up early, did my hair, and finally put on some real clothes. I was a little nervous; however, it was refreshing, and I was finally feeling empowered.

You'd be surprised at the amount of gratitude you can find in the little things when coming from an empty place. A sense of purpose was missing for me. Maybe you feel the same. If so, I encourage you to get up and just find something new to do. Seek whatever new contribution to the world that has your name written all over it—a new hobby, a new job—you choose, as long as getting up is your main priority. "Move a muscle, change a thought" is a well-known sobriety slogan I was told once before. It made perfect sense, and it really does hold its meaning. I urge you to try it. Choose to feel good again because you deserve it. It's time to move a muscle and create some new thoughts. Get back out there again. It's time to fill up your own tank. I want you to know that whatever you choose, YOU. GOT. THIS! No matter what. No matter how big or small. Just like me, you're on your way.

UNPLUGGED

Whether on the job or at home, when any of our electrical devices are in error and fail to work at its full capacity, we dial customer service to request troubleshooting support, right? Usually, the first question a representative will ask is, "Have you tried unplugging your device or applying a forced restart?" Most of the time, that quick resolution does the job. The device restarts, and it resumes functioning at its's expected speed and ability.

Although we aren't electrical devices, we are indeed programmed like one. Sometimes, all we really need is a restart, reboot, or just simply to be unplugged for a moment.

I remember one early Sunday morning, I jolted out of my sleep. For some reason, I had ended up on the floor right next to my bed. As I went to kneel, my back suddenly felt like it weighed a ton, and my chest felt as if it had been packed with multiple needles. I was overcome with anxiety and had a full on anxiety attack. A major one to be exact.

In that very moment, I didn't know what to do or who to call. Nobody would have answered anyway because it was about 4 o'clock in the morning. The only person I thought to call on was God. I was dealing with an unfamiliar error, and I was in need of real support to troubleshoot.

Crying and pleading, I begged, "God, please help me! Something isn't right. Help me, please." The attack came on even stronger, and I felt like I couldn't breathe. I actually thought I was going to die. I pleaded some more and prayed even harder. After a few minutes of pure hell, I managed to talk myself down. The pain in my chest had subsided, but I just couldn't stop crying. I sat on my floor and literally talked to God for about ten minutes straight. I cried, begged, and begged some more. I needed Him to give me some strength, clarity, and a restart to it all.

A good cry is always good to have here and there. It's another form of cleansing. Facing overwhelming anxiety can be so extreme that you may not know how to handle it alone. There have been so many times I cried in the dark, hurt and alone with thoughts that I wasn't going to make it. When you are so strong, you manage stress differently. However, I pray if you're ever faced with such a huge amount of anxiety and stress that you call on God, and He will provide you the strength and reboot that's really needed. You are going to be all right. You are going to make it through!

7

FINDING YOUR PURPOSE WHILE PROTECTING YOUR PEACE

"Thank You, God—for Your blessings, Your mercy, Your Grace, and Your protection."

Anonymous

That whole year had been a farrago for me; however, I needed it. I needed to learn some things about myself I didn't really know. I needed to learn to appreciate some things I had totally taken for granted. I needed to learn that sometimes losing everything really isn't a loss but rather a sign that God was just helping me clean house. I needed to become grateful for the many lessons that turned out to be my biggest blessings.

One thing I truly took from it all was that my spirit had been damaged but certainly not broken. Through it all, I still held on tightly to optimism.

Today, know that doing all the work is hard, but trusting the process is necessary. Things may even get worse before they turn around for your good. Use the constant delays to master your commitments and determine your goals. Don't give up; keep on going.

I challenge you to decide today that you will do whatever it takes to heal yourself. Love yourself. Accept yourself, unconditionally. Flaws and all. Speak life over yourself, and never feel guilty for doing whatever it is that's best for you.

COMING FOR IT ALL!

A different level of strength was required to pull myself out of the deep, dark hole I was in. I'm proud of the woman I am today because I went through so much to become her. Painfully, I really did. Yet, I'm still doing the work, habitually.

I'm almost certain that there will be a lifetime battle involving minor anti-depressive spills, so I won't lie or mislead you into thinking my depression just magically disappeared because it didn't. Some days, that monster still knocks at my door. However, I'm just no longer there to answer. I'm in a happier, more spiritual state. I'm much more conscious and certainly more grateful for the little things daily. Appreciating all of the little things is what prevents me from answering when the monster of depression knocks—the most important such as breath and the ability to wake up, see, and hear. Now, I won't say that gratitude alone is the key to ignoring depression because I'm sure it isn't. That has just been my overall highlight, along with the daily routine of Worship and music to help me maintain.

I'd been working hard. I've been working on myself and maintaining regular self-care routines, such as reciting positive affirmations, getting facials, getting my hair and nails done, and treating myself to something new on a weekly basis. I've been investing in my health with healthier diets and daily exercise, as well as spiritual alignment through reading scriptures and going to church. I've been learning from my solitude through sitting alone, meditating, and utilizing singing bowls. I highly recommend you start seeking and applying some similar routines, if you haven't already. It's very beneficial.

I've been reborn and renewed, and I've had a spiritual awakening. I was intangible and proclaimed that I am the property of God, and depression could no longer trespass. I was ready to take it all back—my family, my mind, my joy, my peace, my love—everything that was meant for me!

Sometimes, way more than often, I wish we didn't have to struggle. I wish we knew it all and had the option to skip through our hardest days, but we can't. What I've learned is that struggle builds character. Struggle builds strength. It may not always look or feel like it, but be encouraged. You survived the days you swore you couldn't! Keep striving, and take back your joy, your peace, and all of your better days!

A MISSING PIECE

One thing I found is that my greatest asset has been learning how to enjoy my own company. I found comfort in being alone. It's a beautiful thing to master. Nonetheless, while on my self-care journey, I've discovered that life is this huge puzzle with unlimited little pieces.

I was putting the pieces of my puzzle together and had figured a huge piece had actually been found: my brother's love.

On this journey, we all are over-qualified, capable, and well-equipped, yet we are also in need of help sometimes to see and understand along our way. My brother had become that help for me.

For quite some time, our bond was loosely held and a disconnection had forcefully occurred long before. Despite that, a full circle of life had come back around. This time, we were evolving together and becoming as "thick as thieves." We pretty much became "sibling goals," and I was very much grateful for that.

From our matching t-shirts and our group chats to our music sessions and the way we just simply understood each other, I was thankful to have him there and close. He had no idea, but he was teaching me how to actually care, laugh, and trust again. Through my toughest progression, he'd become my closest friend.

My brother had faithfully made known that I wasn't in this thing alone, and to be honest, I truly needed that. I needed someone to simply be there.

You'll find that the best kind of support system consists of those who consistently show up—not to fix anything or to do anything in particular but just to let us feel that we are cared for and supported. Rather it's your sibling or not, make sure that if and when you recognize your "missing puzzle piece," you cherish, nurture, appreciate, and hold him or her close. For there's nothing more uplifting than having someone show up and be a vessel in your growth.

NEW GROWTH

Somewhere along the way I decided to do the "big chop." I cut about twelve to fourteen inches of my hair. It was refreshing and free. My new growth and curl pattern had started to flourish really quickly. It was healthy, shiny, and thick. Symbolically, I had rid myself of past pain by cutting off all that dead weight. Together, my hair and I were glowing and growing.

Such a drastic change in hair is known to reflect a subconscious wish for change. When we wish to turn the pages to a new chapter in life, we often start with our head. Perhaps a change in color or even growing or shaving a beard for some men. There is a strong and often apparent link between character, mood, and hair. The well-known fashionista Coco Chanel even said, "A woman who cuts her hair is planning changes in her life." I started taking inventory of my own and had planned a whole list of changes. My wish is that you, too, have decided to do the same.

My question to you now is are you ready? Ready for that drastic change? Ready for your "big chop"? If not, I urge you to get ready. Cut off all the dead weight. Period. Let go of anyone or anything that disrupts your growth and/or does not assist in the attainment of your goals.

BAD HABITS & OPEN DOORS

It's amazing what a fresh perspective can do. Viewing change from both your own and another's point-of-view allows you the ability to find understanding in reasoning. But first, you have to be willing to become more open-mind to doing so. I was in such a healthy state of mind that I was able to see things completely and differently. I started to find deeper meanings in it all—numbers, quotes, things, and even people. New doors and signs were appearing at a blink of an eye. Bad habits were changing, and when one door closed, I was already knocking at another one. I was gaining clarity, and my fuel tanks were on full.

It all reminds me of the song, "I can see clearly now, the rain is gone" because that's exactly what it was. The storm had passed. I wasn't just surviving anymore. I was thriving. I had learned that breaking huge challenges down into smaller ones was the best method toward achievement. I had fully comprehended that my desires and intentions were way more than just me. I moved myself and my son out of public housing and didn't need to rely on government assistance anymore. I was doing well. I found a place big enough to even open my door to one of my younger cousins who was seeking guidance and the same level of peace, which I prayed upon us all.

Things were really turning around. Had I not shut out all distractions and became focused, none of this would have been possible. Seeing all that did happen was way too important to me though!

You have to get to the point where you desire to be so focused, you shut the doors to all distractions—social media, your phone, your family—and you just get focused. You have to make the commitment to stay away from meaningless distractions to gain the life you deserve. You will remain empty inside, chasing and entertaining things that aren't important because you aren't feeding your soul. You're just contaminating it. I want you to understand there is a pride that comes from self-growth. There is growth from putting your needs and wants first and from finding a way when it seems as if there's no way out at all. There is growth that comes when you go beyond the life you once thought was unattainable. Know that every day you decide to choose anything over yourself and your own goals, you form a bad habit—a habit that gets stronger and makes you weaker. It defeats your wildest dreams and stagnates your overall growth.

I challenge you to form a different habit. A habit of discipline. A habit to commit to what's truly important. A habit to go all in for putting your dreams first. A habit of integrity. A habit to open some new doors.

INCREASING HAPPINESS TO JOY

It was in the little ones' laugher, personalities, and curiosity that I found my most joy—especially with my girls. My niece was the main one. Our bond was different from with my boys. She just knew how to make my heart really feel. She was my girl, and she knew it.

Outside of my son being the center of my life, my niece, my nephew, and my God-daughters meant the most to me. I didn't think I could ever love another like my own, but they all proved me wrong. Each had their own special reason, and altogether they made me feel whole. Honestly, they were another reason to just be.

A lot of times, I'd have them all over just because. They'd assist with increasing my emotional tank to overflow a little more. We would be "mad lit" as my nephew would say with his big, bright smile. I value being the best mom, the favorite aunt, and a great God-parent. They made me happy, and I laughed A LOT! Observing them interact with one another and eavesdropping on their interesting conversations was my favorite thing to do though. Although they were these tiny, little beings, they actually taught me a lot—patience for sure but most of all, how to love.

The main key here is to discover what or who it is that can be of assistance when increasing your emotional tank. It doesn't have to necessarily be kids who help you when doing so. Maybe this sort of positive impact may come from your friends, siblings (if any), and/or a significant other. What I hope is that you'll recognize and cherish an overflow of genuine love.

One of the biggest realizations I've found is that I'm actually learning how to love. I never realized that I didn't know how to love—at least not in the healthy and appropriate way. My babies have helped me live up to the truth I didn't even realize I was avoiding, which has resulted in many differences I, personally, can attest to now.

That brought me much happiness!

What is it that is really increases your happiness? This may seem like a simple question however I'm challenging you to seek beyond the surface answer. What brings you happiness that truly fulfills your joy. Because the two are in fact different. I found happiness in the kids but it's within learning to love again that I gain sustainable joy.

PIVOTING TO PURPOSE

I knew it was time for me to pivot to my purpose when I started doing just enough at work, not to get fired. To find your purpose in life, you have to ask yourself what it is and who do you passionately desire to help? When you discover your what, it becomes much easier to find your why.

There was something in me that couldn't settle no more. Something in me that constantly irritates me and reminds me "this can't be it." I kept telling myself that there has to be more. I had to be created for a much bigger purpose than playing so small.

I'm praying writing be it; throughout these words I pray; I help to knock down some barriers for many people who haven't found that confidence in themselves to do it alone. Perhaps even just to be the one, chosen to be the cycle breaker in my own family. The one that keeps fighting the good fight and demands "these generational curses shall end with me."

You see we all have the power in each of us to do more, manifest and create our own destiny. It's time I create mine. Whatever it is that I really want, I'm making the commitment to myself to be steadfast and to really give it my all.

I have always had the passion to influence and encourage; even with my disadvantages I can only hope that my words are truly felt and loudly heard. I hope you to, find what it is your called to do. For we are all born to take up space and to leave our mark. Seek and you shall find; ask and you shall be given.

My wish is that you find yourself, happiness and much joy and While on that journey your purpose just happens to find its merry way to you.

SIGNED, SEALED...NOW DELIVER

I want to share my final thoughts with you. I want to challenge you just one last time. I want you to take some time and really sit with yourself. While sitting with yourself, I want you to build some courage to write a letter to the hurting, vulnerable, scared, innocent, and youngest version of yourself.

While I still have you as my beloved audience, I'd like to share a few things I would say to the younger version of myself as well.

Dear Little One,

I'm sorry!

I'm sorry it took so long for me to look for you after all these years. I was looking for love in so many different places and never realized you were always there. I'm sorry I blamed you for so much of this pain. Please know it's not your fault, and it never has been. All the heartbreaks, confusion, and nights you had to cry alone—I'm sorry for the many goodbyes and all the boys who ever lied.

I'm sorry for the people who took you for granted and for all the apologies you'll never receive but that you most definitely deserve.

I need you to know that [in this life] you are going to have a lot of days when you don't feel accepted, protected, or complete. There will even be times when you are actually going to feel less than. I want you to know that you're enough. You are loved. You are honored. You are whole.

You are beautiful, and you're made perfectly imperfect. You are unique, and you are a gorgeous, strong Black queen. There may be girls who seem to be praised more than you, but that's not true. Your skin is dark, but you shine so bright. You are important, and you have a purpose in this world. Daddy may not have been there to show you he cares or remind you of your worth, but Little One, I wanted to be the one to tell you, personally, that you are priceless and worthy of it all! Please don't cry. Don't even be sad. Daddy didn't love you enough because he didn't even know how to love himself. Forgive him!

You're going to meet a monster that lives inside of you. Its name is depression, and it's going to feel so big. It doesn't have you, you have it—along with a mighty God who is even bigger than the monster. He will always see you through. He won't ever forsake you or give you any more than you can bear. Be sure to keep your faith high. It is going to be hard, and you may even want to give up. Don't! Keep going. Fight a good fight!

Grow, and when you get there grow some more. Reach high, even when you're feeling mighty low. Don't be so hard on yourself. Struggles and mistakes are meant to shape and mold you into the courageous woman you'll become.

Be fearless. Love hard, even when it hurts. Know when to let go. For everything isn't meant to be. Show up and stand out because you weren't created to fit in. Be unapologetic, transparent, and don't run from your truth!

Be free, grounded, and confident when you walk.

Be kind to yourself and all those around you; for it's a cold world out there. Be a friend and the person you once needed. You'll touch a lot of hearts and make a lot of people smile, and you still might feel alone. You are not. I am with you. I promise you, I am here. Keep being you. Always be true, and know that nobody else loves you like I do!

Love,
Your Future Self

I want to thank God for EVERYTHING—my strength, my vision, and for guiding me through it all!

To my son, I want you to believe deep in your heart that YOU are more than capable of achieving ANYTHING you put your mind to. Believe there is no such thing as a loser—either you win or you learn. Remember to ALWAYS aim for the sky—for the sky's the limit. I can't promise to be here for the rest of your life, but I can promise to LOVE YOU deeply for the rest of mine!

Love, Mom

Special dedication goes to my brother—you are the main vessel who helped me to love again. In my darkest moments, you were the rays of light that I truly needed. I thank God for you! I love you to the moon and back. Don't you ever forget that! When nobody else is there, I'll be by your side. Always!

To Auntie's baby (Taier), my fat girl (Saraii), and both of my God-Babies (Desire & A'riiya): I thank all four of you for filling my voids and making my heart much, much warmer! I LOVE YOU all as my very own! Never give up on your dreams or, most importantly, YOURSELVES.

Always remember: whenever and however,
I am here to help!

xoxo

An abundance of gratitude, yet few words are adequate enough:

However, to the entire D.O.P.E. Publishing team, especially my editor, Meloni Williams, for giving me a chance, taking her time, guiding and supporting me through this whole process—step-by-step—and helping my book reach its greatest potential.

I TRULY THANK YOU!

NOTES

Chapter 1

1. https://www.biblegateway.com/passage/?search=proverbs+15%3A4&version=ESV
2. https://www.biblegateway.com/passage/?search=proverbs+16%3A24&version=ESV
3. https://www.biblegateway.com/passage/?search=Luke+23%3A34&version=ESV